MAKE THE BEST
of the Rest

BILL MICKLER

Published by Insight International, Inc.
contact@freshword.com
www.freshword.com
918-493-1718

ISBN: 978-1-943361-57-1
E-Book ISBN: 978-1-943361-58-8

Library of Congress Control Number: 2019905450

Printed in the United States of America.

DEDICATION

I dedicate this book to my beautiful wife, Pam, who is truly a precious gift from God.

You believed in me when I didn't believe in myself. I would not be the man I am today without your unconditional love and encouragement. I love you!

CONTENTS

FOREWORD

Decide to do something today that your future self will thank you for—read Bill Mickler's new book, *Make the Best of the Rest.*

I'm honored to call Bill my friend. I've experienced firsthand God's wisdom through him in my own life. Now you can too.

I promise his book will show you how to hear from the Holy Spirit and rightfully discover His plan and purpose for your life...from this moment forward.

The good news is God can change things right now, right here, where you are. No matter your current circumstances.

Some of the best days of your life haven't yet happened. That's why this book is so valuable. No longer let mistakes and disappointments of the past control and direct your future.

Just because something hasn't worked out for you now, doesn't mean there's not something big in store for you in the future. Now, through the wisdom in this book, discover God's best from this day forward.

–John Mason
Author of *An Enemy Called Average* and
numerous other best-selling books

ACKNOWLEDGEMENTS

A special thanks to best-selling author, John Mason, for his "nuggets." They were awesome and really helped this first-time writer. (Find it hard to say author.) I highly recommend John's *The Ultimate Author Tool*. It was excellent!

Michelle Mason, you were so helpful in getting me through the publishing process. You are a delight to work with. Insight International is a great organization.

Dr. Thelma Snuggs, you were so good to assist with the editing of this book. Thanks for the hours you gave.

Sandy Marchel, you were always available to help coordinate and assist with my totally inadequate computer skills. Thank you.

Pam Mickler, my beautiful wife, your constant encouragement, input, and special notes to me were what made this book become a reality. Your editing was fantastic! Let's do it again.

A special thanks to Pastor Billy Joe Daugherty, who now resides in heaven. Your love for people and your messages changed my life.

Pastor Sharon Daugherty, thank you for the endorsement of this book. Your love for people and your messages have also changed my life. I thank God for leading me to Victory Christian Center in Tulsa, Oklahoma.

INTRODUCTION

It is my hope this book will encourage, exhort and edify you to fulfill your God given destiny during your time on earth.

No matter what you have experienced in your life up to this point, there is still more for you to accomplish and to enjoy...all bringing glory to God.

Our time on earth is limited, and only what we accomplish for the glory of God will accompany us into eternity. It is there, in Heaven, with God, that we will receive our ultimate reward. What an exciting day that will be.

No matter how many times we fail God, He will never fail us. God wants to reveal to you His plan, and He will continually be with you throughout this exciting journey.

The Bible refers to the life span of man as 120 years. I believe most of us look at 100 years as being a full life. Regardless of your thoughts, here is an example below for you to check to see where you are in your earthly life span, but please remember that when we finish our time here, we are headed to heaven to live eternally with Jesus.

100 Year Life Span (A Goal for Many)	120 Year Life Span (Genesis 6:3)
0 25..............1st Quarter	0-30............1st Quarter
26-50..........2nd Quarter	31-60..........2nd Quarter
51-75..........3rd Quarter	61-90..........3rd Quarter
76-100........4th Quarter	91-120........4th Quarter

How many years do you have left on your earth life cycle? Are you ready to:

"MAKE THE BEST OF THE REST"

1

WHAT HAPPENED?

"Your divorce has been granted and is now final."

I really thought I was prepared for what I soon discovered I was totally unprepared for. I was granted by a judge what I never really wanted, and yet I was the one who made the request.

As you look back over your life, can you relate to this? You pursued something that in your right mind you would never have pursued. Then you ultimately get what you pursued, only then wondering why you pursued it.

Sometimes it appears that life can be full of contradictions. We have all had similar type experiences. Pursuing something we thought we wanted, only to eventually come to our senses and truly realize that the thing pursued was not really what we wanted.

In a brief moment of time I made a decision that would have serious ramifications for years to come for a family that I dearly loved. It was a heartbreaking time in my life, and it was one of the darkest moments in my life.

Maybe you have experienced similar types of heartbreaking periods in your life, times when darkness seemed to surround you. Maybe even at this moment you are going through one of those times.

I can assure you that you are going to eventually be alright, but there are times when we must press on in spite of devastating circumstances, some caused by ourselves, some caused by others, some by a combination of both.

There is always hope, but at that time in my life, I had no hope. I certainly didn't know the Author of hope. I'll share more on hope in another chapter.

All I knew for sure at this period in my life was that I had drifted into the things the world had to offer, and the dark period in my life was getting much, much darker. As I reflect back on that period, I find it difficult to believe I did many of the foolish things I did. It was not a good time, and it seemed to last forever.

Over the years in ministry I have met many people with similar devastating experiences, and there seems to be a common bond. This bond is, that regardless of how difficult the challenge was, it is possible to go on with life with a deep emotional scar. It is possible to move on with God realizing that the scar may remain, but the healing power of God will be there for us.

The important thing is to make a decision to never give up. God will eventually bring us through. No matter what you are currently facing, no matter how difficult the circumstances, you are going to be alright.

God is a good God, and He always wants to heal us and show us the future He has for us. He will never leave or forsake us. He will always be there for us. He loves us, and He wants the very best for us.

Throughout the chapters of this book we will share experiences from God's word, from actual experiences of the miracle working power of God in the lives of people, and the miracles I have seen God perform in restoring my life.

The miracle working power doesn't always work the way we think it will, but the miracle working power of restoration works according to God's will. It is His love for us that always gives us hope for the future.

No matter what your past has been, good bad or ugly, I guarantee God has a wonderful future for you. He loves you, and all He wants in return is for you to love Him. His gift of His love to the world is truly His greatest gift. He will take every negative experience you have ever encountered and turn it around.

"All things work together for good to those who love God and are called according to His purpose."

(ROMANS 8:28)

Do you love God? Are you called according to His purpose? If the answer is yes, then you are ready to:

"MAKE THE BEST OF THE REST"

2

MAKING A BAD SITUATION WORSE

Have you ever decided to take matters into your own hands and fix things?

This is what my brilliant mind decided to do. Now that everything I ever wanted was broken and shattered into pieces, a terrible mess...I would fix it all. (Guess I never learned from the nursery rhyme of Humpty Dumpty.)

Well, as you can probably imagine, this didn't work out very well. (That is an extreme understatement.) Have you ever tried to fix something that you couldn't fix? That was my plan. I didn't know Jesus yet, but I was on a mission to fix whatever was broken.

It didn't take too long to realize that in my brilliance, I had turned a really bad situation into a disaster. I have heard it said that when you have dug a big hole for yourself, you should just stop digging. Well, I just kept on digging.

In a relatively short period of time of trying to fix every-thing, I had moved from my home to an apartment, back to my home, only to return to the apartment again, and then repeat the process over and over again. I think I might have been going crazy in the process in addition to driving everyone involved a little crazy.

In addition to all of this, I began to drink fairly heavily. I had two businesses that I was neglecting badly. My life was truly spiraling out of control, and either I didn't know it or I didn't care. I'm not sure which.

If you have ever tried to fix something that apparently can't be fixed (and I am relatively certain you have), you know the feeling. You don't realize it at the time because you're busy trying to fix the problem, but you soon can relate to Don Quixote in *The Man From La Mancha* when he finally realized he was no match for the windmill.

Eventually, when we are facing circumstances we can't fix, we can sometimes try even harder, making a really bad situation worse for everyone. That was certainly my situation. Maybe you too have "been there and done that."

In my case I even added to the equation of fixing the problem…frustration, anger, resentment, unforgiveness, and alcohol. Talk about ingredients for disaster! I was an explosion in the making with a lit fuse.

How about you? What are you facing? I learned my lesson the hard way. I didn't realize there was a God that I could turn to who would help me. I thought I had to do it all myself. What are you trying to fix yourself?

My life was going downhill fast, but it was about to change. I was about to be confronted by a least likely individual who was going to be used mightily by God to not only change my life, but to save my life.

I was about to learn that I couldn't fix the past or change the present, but I could certainly:

"MAKE THE BEST OF THE REST"

3

THE GREATEST BOOK ON POSITIVE THINKING EVER WRITTEN

During my infamous period of frustration and drifting, I had purchased a business and hired a lady named Jean to be my secretary and receptionist.

A nice lady about fifteen years older than me. I had worked with her years before when I was in the management program at the J.C. Penney Company. I'm always fascinated how God will use different people to influence and impact our lives.

The people you associate with and the books you read will ultimately have the potential to be your dominant influence. This is why I believe, as many others do, that you will always be greatly impacted in all of your decisions in life based on the books you read and the people you associate with. Both have tremendous potential to impact your life.

How are you in this arena? What books do you read and who do you continually associate with? Do they bring out the best in you? Do they motivate you, or do they continually have to be motivated? There is nothing wrong with being around people who need to be motivated. I love the opportunity to motivate people, but don't forget to have an inner circle of people who bring out the best in you and motivate you.

Back to my new employee, Jean, at my business. I didn't realize it at the time I hired her, but she was about to be used by God to change my life…actually, a better description would be that she was about to be used by God to save my life. I believe Jean was assigned to me by God.

I must admit that at that at the time when she began her God given assignment, I thought I had made a mistake in hiring her and that she was becoming a pain in the _____. (You know!)

There are people who God has assigned to intervene in our lives that at first may seem to be somewhat threatening and intimidating, maybe even a little overbearing. When these people surface in our lives, we need to swallow our pride and let them complete their God given assignment.

It was very difficult for me to allow Jean to impart into my life, but I know now, without a doubt, God used her to save my life. I will be eternally grateful.

Don't miss your opportunity to entertain someone assigned by God to be a blessing to you, and don't miss an opportunity to be used by God to be a blessing to someone. I guarantee you, once God is allowed to intervene in your life and fix you, He will launch you out into the deep of hurting humanity to help others.

"Launch out into the deep and let down your nets for a catch. Do not be afraid. From now on you will catch men."

(LUKE 5:4 AND LUKE 5:10)

By the time I hired Jean I was the owner of now two businesses, drinking heavily, and working my way into a debt of approximately $30,000 trying to act like all was well while sinking deeper and deeper into the abyss of disappointment, discouragement, and depression.

Have you been there? Maybe you are there now. Don't give up! Help is on the way! What God did for me, He will also do for you. God will rescue anyone who is open to His intervention. I wasn't very open at first, but He never gave up and I finally gave in. A great combination for success.

I had always been what I thought was a very positive, confident person prior to my life disintegrating before my very eyes. Nothing I did seemed to help. My background training as a Marine, a management leader at the J. C. Penney Co., or a District Manager for a large restaurant franchise chain had not prepared me for what I was facing: A failed marriage, disappointing three beautiful children that I loved, and now financial disaster.

My secret thought during this period: "What is there to live for?"

Maybe you're in a similar situation. Hang in there, because God is on the horizon. He's going to come to your rescue, just as He rescued me. God has ordained victory for your future, and He does not fail!

My life was about to change, and regardless of what you are facing, or will ever face, God will be there for you. I didn't realize it, but I was about to experience the biggest miracle of my life.

The day that set in motion the eventual day that would change my life forever began like most days. I arrived at my office and began to browse through the mail, when I noticed a new book laying on my desk.

I love all books, but especially new ones. As I opened the first page, I saw an inscription on the inside:

Bill,

This is the greatest book on positive thinking ever written.

Jean

I was always meeting with our staff sharing with them on the power of positive thinking. Two of my favorite books were Norman Vincent Peale's *The Power of Positive Thinking* and Zig Ziglar's *See You at the Top.*

I had just recently taken our entire staff to a positive thinking conference at the old Market Square Arena in Indianapolis with the keynote speaker being Zig Ziglar, a great motivational speaker.

Needless to say, I was excited to have another new book on the power of positive thinking, even though none of them appeared to be helping me. It always intrigued me that during that time of my life, I still wanted to help other people succeed even though I had seemingly given up on myself.

Back to my office and my new book and the temporary joy I felt: A new book on positive thinking!

As I turned from the first page with the inscription from Jean to the cover, I saw a man with a boy on his shoulders apparently to project the image of a father and his son.

The picture for some unexplained reason really penetrated the emotions of my heart along with what was embossed on the cover: *The Greatest Gift Is Love.* I wasn't sure what that meant, but the wording seemed to fit the intent of the picture.

I can still remember the warm feeling in my heart when I actually opened the book to check out the content. I was really surprised, shocked might be a better word, when I realized it was apparently a Bible in disguise.

I remember vividly throwing the book over on the edge of the credenza behind my desk and thinking the following: "Damn it, I wish she (Jean) would leave me alone."

Jean had recently received Jesus into her heart at the First Assembly of God church, and she had been trying to tell me about it for several weeks. Apparently, she thought it was her job now to tell me all about Jesus. Well, as far as I was concerned, it wasn't! It was fine for her, but I just wanted her to leave me alone!

Jean was becoming a giant pain in the _____. (No, not neck.)

Sometimes when she was trying to tell me about Jesus, I would just tell her to go back to her desk and get some work done. Often, she was reluctant to do that, so I would use a few choice words to get her out of my office. I was beginning to regret ever hiring her.

On more than one occasion she would tear up after I told her what I thought about her religion and Jesus. I wasn't brought up in church and I had never read the Bible. I find it hard to believe that I treated her the way I did, and I find it even harder to believe that she continued to take my abuse. I don't know how she did it, but I thank God she never let go of her assignment.

Even to this day I have to be careful to not let my old self utter a few choice words when things aren't going the way I think they should. Unfortunately, some of the people in our church know this.

One of our members recently gave me a wall plaque for my office:

"I love Jesus, I just cuss a little."

Back again to the book (Bible), that I threw in the corner of my office credenza.

I had arrived this day and the office was empty. Sitting at my desk starring straight ahead I began to think about everything that had been happening in my life. My world was continuing to fall apart at a rapid speed, and apparently there was nothing I could do to stop it. I was frustrated, unhappy, worried, anxious, and extremely disappointed with myself.

It was as if the entire weight of the world had fallen on me. If it wasn't for my three children, who I loved so much, I don't think I would have really cared if I lived or died. It's hard to describe, but I felt my life was being sucked out of me, and I really didn't care.

I don't know how long I sat at my desk motionless, but eventually I looked over toward my credenza and noticed the book with the picture of what I identified in my heart as a loving father with his son on his shoulders.

For a moment it brought back wonderful memories of the times when I would hoist one of my children on my shoulders. I guess you could call it a memory flash back…very pleasant. I'm always amazed at how in just a moment a wonderful memory from the past can penetrate your heart and mind and overpower your emotions resulting in uncontrollable tears of joy.

As I picked up the book, still thinking about my children and the love I had for them and the joy that they were to me, I noticed a small notation to turn to a certain page on love. As I did I realized it was a step by step numbering system taking you to several scriptures sharing God's love for mankind. It was really interesting, something I had never thought about. Not only did I not know God loved us, I didn't even know there was a God.

There is a great line in the movie *Forrest Gump:* "Stupid is as stupid does." I find it hard to believe that in the days I am now describing, I was totally ignorant of the things of God, and worse yet, totally ignorant that there was a God.

I hadn't heard Jean arrive at the office, and, didn't realize she was there until she looked around the corner of my office wall and noticed my reading the book.

At first she startled me, and then for some unexplained reason I felt a little embarrassed.

Jean spoke first, "It's a great book."

By then I had followed the numbers through the basic love scriptures.

"It would be nice if it were true," was my quiet, not normal, subdued response.

Jean just stood in the doorway for what seemed an eternity.

"Would you have lunch with a businessman from my church?"

I couldn't believe my response, "Sure, why not."

That businessman took me to lunch and later took me to his church. His name was Joe, and all he wanted to do was talk about all the things Jesus had done in his life. It was a fascinating story he told me of his life before Jesus, and all the miracles Jesus had done for him.

I don't think I totally understood everything he was sharing, but the one thing I was certain of was that he was really different. I couldn't describe what that meant, but I knew I had never met anyone like him. He had something I didn't have, and even though I didn't know what it was, I think I thought I might want it.

That doesn't really make any sense, but it truly describes what was happening.

When we arrived at his church he took me to the pastor's office, but he was in another area doing a recording for the church media. He was scheduled to return shortly so his secretary asked us to wait in his office.

Reflecting back on what all was happening that day, I thank God that my new friend Joe was not in a hurry. He spent about an hour and a half with me at lunch, and now was going to continue spending time with me awaiting the arrival of the pastor.

Sometimes we can all get in a hurry with life and miss the most important assignment God has for us at that moment of that day. I thank God Jean never got in a hurry with me, and I thank God Joe was not in a hurry with me.

As we sat in the pastor's office with Joe sharing story after story with me of what God had done in his life, he suddenly stopped, looked me directly in the eye and asked me if I was ready to receive Jesus as my Lord and Savior.

I still can't believe it, but I heard this word come out my mouth instantly: "Yes."

"Yes" is what I said, but what I thought right after I said yes was: "Why not, nothing else seems to be working?"

Joe led me in the prayer and confession asking Jesus to come into my life, forgive me of my sins, and acknowledging Him as the Son of God. I must admit I really didn't understand what all was going on, but I knew something was happening and I was not in control. It was something much, much bigger than me.

I believe our most important assignment from God is to tell people about Jesus, and I am so thankful Joe was willing to spend time with me and lead me to the Son of God, who would change my life for eternity. Both Joe and Jean are in heaven now, but I am so thankful they were willing to let God use them to save my life.

If you know Jesus as your Lord and Savior, God wants to use you to intervene in the lives of other people, especially those who have never accepted Jesus as their Lord and Savior, or those who have walked away from Him. If you have Jesus, then you are permanently on assignment to share the love of Jesus with people everywhere you go. The power to change a life is in you if you know Jesus.

It was that day that changed my life for eternity, and it was in part because two people were willing to share their time, their love, and the love of God's Son with me, enabling me to:

"MAKE THE BEST OF THE REST"

Perhaps you have never accepted Jesus as your Lord and Savior, or maybe you once served Him, but you know you have slipped away from the relationship you once had. Why not accept him into your heart right now. It is always the right time to do the right thing by accepting Jesus.

Just pray this prayer of confession:

"Jesus, I believe You are the Son of God. I believe you died for my sins and rose again. I have sinned and I have made mistakes, but today I acknowledge You as my Lord and Savior. I ask You to come into my heart and take control of

my life. The true desire of my heart is to serve You and to be all you have called me to be."

If you just prayed that prayer, I congratulate you. You are now ready to serve God and fulfill your God given destiny on this earth. Find a church that teaches and preaches the power of the word of God and the leading of the Holy Spirit.

Now your life will be changed for eternity, just as mine was, and you are ready to:

"MAKE THE BEST OF THE REST"

4

THE IMPORTANCE OF HOPE

It is hard to describe what happened to me the minute I received Jesus as My Lord and Savior, but I think the best way I can state it is that everything was now different. It was as if I were living in a different world.

People looked different, the sky was different, the air was different, trees were different…it was as if with my eyes and my natural senses I was seeing the world through a different focus…and I liked it, whatever it was.

I can say that for the first time in my life, I felt hope, but it was not a natural hope. It was something beyond natural. Only much later did I really realize what had actually happened. My spirit man had been born again, and now I was a different person.

In the beginning when God created man, we were created to be a three part being: Spirit, Soul and Body. When sin entered into the world when Adam and Eve disobeyed God, the spirit of man died. Instead of man being a three part being, he became a two part being. This continued until Jesus came as God's master plan to take away the sins of all mankind and birth forth our spirit man in all of those who would accept Jesus as their Lord and Savior.

> *"But of the tree of the knowledge of good and evil you shall not eat, for in the day that you eat of it you shall surely die."*
>
> (GENESIS 2:17)

> *"Most assuredly, I say to you, unless a man is born again, he cannot see the kingdom of God."*
>
> (JOHN 3:3)

> *"That which is born of flesh is flesh, and that which is born of the Spirit is Spirit."*
>
> (JOHN 3:6)

In the book of John, Jesus is describing to one of the Jewish Rabbis the tremendous importance of being born again by receiving Jesus Christ as our Lord and Savior. The Rabbi, Nicodemus, a ruler of the Jews, was asking Jesus to explain what the born again experience really meant.

When our spirit man is born again the way of God's original intent, we truly become a new person, referred to in the Bible as a new creation. It isn't something that we understand at first, because it is something that happens in the realm of the spirit.

It was always God's will from the beginning that man would be led by his spirit following the leading of God's Holy Spirit. I didn't know any of this in the beginning, but one thing I knew for sure, I now had hope.

It wasn't that I had hope for my previous marriage or anything specific, I just had hope that I had a future. Again, it is something that was very hard for me to describe, but I knew that no matter what I had experienced, or would ever experience, there was hope. I'm not even sure I knew what hope meant.

Here is the Bible definition for hope in the Greek language:

Hope: (Elpis)
Confident expectation with a sure foundation.

This sounds like a funny statement, but at that time in my life I didn't know what I had, but I knew I had it.

I know the feeling of hopelessness, and I hate it. After spending almost forty years in ministry, I understand how destructive hopelessness is. I know that once we can get a person's hopes up, we can begin to make a difference in their lives through the Name of Jesus and the power of the Holy Spirit.

"Hope deferred makes the heart sick, But when desire comes it is a tree of life."

(PROVERBS 13:12)

There is a somewhat popular saying in the world that is totally contrary to the word of God when it comes to hope, and that saying is:

"Don't get your hopes up!"

I believe most people who say that think they are protecting someone from getting their feelings hurt or from being disappointed. Personally, I believe it is a tactic from the devil to do the exact opposite of what God would have us to do.

God wants us to get our hopes up in Him, and, keep them up. Just look at some of the examples He has given us in His word:

"And now Lord, what do I wait for? My hope is in You!"

(PSALM 39:7)

"For you are my hope, O Lord God; You are my trust from my youth."

(PSALM 70:5)

The word of God specifically tells us that hope in God will never disappoint us. It is one of my favorite scriptures to share with people who are concerned about getting their hopes up only to be disappointed, or the prospect of getting a family member's hopes up or the hopes of a friend. This scripture is found in the Book of Romans:

"Now hope does not disappoint, because the love of God has been poured out in our hearts by the Holy Spirit who was given to us."

(ROMANS 5:5)

What I'm about to share may sound like a contradiction regarding getting your hopes up, but I don't believe it is. I believe it is just a further encouragement to get your hopes up, even when you have been disappointed.

Disappointment is part of life. Sometimes things just don't work out the way we had hoped. The devil loves to play with our mind and tell us this hope stuff just doesn't work. If he can play with our mind and steal our hope, then he will follow up with disappointment, that can lead to discouragement, and these two can easily lead to depression.

I have observed many people over my years in ministry who have been disappointed, allowed that to discourage them, and then eventually entered into full blown depression. Sometimes a person doesn't even know it.

My hope is that what I'm about to share comes across to you through the leading of the Holy Spirit, but my encouragement to you is this: What is the big deal about being disappointed? There isn't a single one of us who hasn't been disappointed in life.

I could list example after example of areas where all of us have been disappointed at one time or another: Our first girl-friend or boyfriend, the bike I wanted as a little boy but never received, a pair of blue suede shoes (I did receive those), the boy to ask me out on a date who never did, the boy who asked me out and I wondered why I ever went, the girl who said she loved me and then dumped me, etc., etc., etc.

The childhood disappointments, however, don't compare to those we experience as adults, and that is why we must learn to deal with them quickly. My method works for me, and I know it will work for you.

First, we must realize that there will be disappointments in life. Therefore, we go through life, not expecting them, but realizing that when they happen we must know how to deal with them.

In other words, when you get knocked down by the power of disappointment, you need to know how to get up quickly to get on with the rest of your life. If you don't do this, there can be a tendency to stay down and feel sorry for yourself. A favorite ploy of the devil...feeling sorry for yourself.

Then if a person stays in that state long enough, they want other people to feel sorry for them. Once this happens you are on a downward spiral on a slippery slope soon to be followed by discouragement and depression.

Sadly, many people never realize their problem. The problem isn't the disappointment...the problem isn't the discourage-ment...the problem isn't the depression...the problem is that they have lost hope!

In our world society today, I believe there are many, many people who are being treated medically when the real treatment that is needed is spiritual. The spirit of man, full of hope in God, renewing the mind to realize that no matter how difficult the disappointment is, we will be alright because we have hope in God and this hope in God will never disappoint us.

We must realize and be prepared that sometimes in life things do not work out the way we had hoped, and we have been, and may be in the future disappointed but we will not stay disappointed. We will focus our attention and our hope in God that we will let go of the disappointment and grab hold of our hope in God. In life on this earth we may be disappointed from time to time, but our God will never disappoint us.

The Biblical story of David and his encounter with disappointment in an area called Ziklag is a great example of how to handle disappointment. It was a devastating experience for David and his men…totally unexpected. One moment everything was fine, and the next moment there was total disappointment.

Let me set the stage for you. David and his loyal fighting men, along with their wives, children, and all their earthly possessions were living in an area called Ziklag. Apparently, David felt led to take his men with him to help the Philistines in an upcoming fight against King Saul and his men.

Upon arriving for the battle, David was informed by the Philistine leadership that they did not want him and his men fighting alongside them in this upcoming fight. They were concerned about David's possible previous loyalty toward King Saul.

David pleaded his case to the Philistine leadership, but to no avail. He and his men were ordered to return to Ziklag, and David obeyed. He and his loyal men departed on a three-day journey to return to their home and family and possessions in Ziklag.

I'm sure David's men were disappointed. They had all been trained as fighting men loyal to their leader, and they were obviously hoping to be victorious in a good fight. But on the other hand, they were all probably excited to return to their wives and children.

As David and his men approached Ziklag they saw that the village had been burned to the ground and all the families and possessions had been taken by the enemy, the Amalekites.

Here is the story unfolding as David and his men went from disappointment, discouragement and depression, to eventually hope in the Lord:

> *"So, David came to the city that had been burned with fire, and the wives, sons and daughters had been taken captive. Then David and his men lifted up their voices and wept until there was no more power to weep. Now David was greatly distressed for his men spoke of stoning him, but David strengthened himself in the Lord his God. David inquired of the Lord what to do, and the Lord answered: 'Pursue, for you shall surely overtake them and without fail you shall recover all.'"*

> (I SAMUEL 30:3-8)

David did exactly as the Lord commanded, and he and his men recovered all, just as the Lord said. In times of bitter disappointment, we must turn immediately to the Lord. He will always give us hope through his command.

In David's case he and his men recovered all and there was total restoration of all that had been taken, and this is always a wonderful thing. I have, however, experienced in my life of ministry, that God is always a God of restoration, but it doesn't always happen the way we think it will.

Our trust, our hope, must be in the Lord. No matter what we are going through, God will take care of us. No matter how devastating the disappointment, God will be there with us, and as long as we have hope in God, we will be alright.

What is the disappointment you are facing? What is your Ziklag experience?

What have you arrived home to discover to your disappointment has gone wrong? What disappointment are you facing that has you right on the slippery edge of discouragement and depression?

With God, you will be alright. He is there with you to help you through whatever the disappointment might be. He still has a plan and a purpose for your life.

Release your hope in God knowing that he has a plan for you to:

"MAKE THE BEST OF THE REST "

5

THE POWER OF ASKING IN PRAYER

The importance of prayer cannot be overemphasized. It will change your life. It will change your spiritual surroundings, and it will open the door for the miracle working power of God to bless you and bring forth His will through your prayers.

I believe that in the simplest of terminology prayer is simply you talking to God and God talking to you, giving you instructions, assurance, and building your faith. The more we talk (prayer) with God, the more we hear from God, and the more we hear from God, the more our faith grows.

"Faith comes by hearing and hearing by the word of God."

(ROMANS 10:17)

No matter what you are currently facing in your life, God is aware, and He is looking forward to meeting your every need. It is through prayer that God gives us instructions, and it is through prayer that we ask God to intervene in our lives. I know that some Biblical scholars may not agree with this, but my experience is that it is true. I believe I have experienced it in my life.

I believe God will allow us to do our own thing, watching and waiting, and hoping (yes, hoping…the Author of hope), hoping we will seek Him, His direction, His counsel. I know this has been true in my life. Some of my biggest challenges since accepting Jesus as my Lord and Savior have come because I did not communicate with God regarding decisions I was making. Doing this is disaster in the making. It is like playing Russian Roulette.

Somehow in the midst of all God was trying to do in my life regarding my future, my business and every other aspect of living, I felt a void. Receiving Jesus as my Lord and Savior was the most awesome experience of my life, but for some reason I felt something was missing.

One evening as I was sitting on the edge of the bed in my apartment, I felt a strong desire to be married again. I hadn't thought about that part of my life. By this time, I knew there was no chance of my previous marriage ever being restored. I was ready to move on with my life with Jesus, but I kept feeling this desire surfacing to follow after Jesus with a wife.

Sitting on the edge of my bed late one evening, I began to think about the desire I had to share the rest of my life with someone, but I knew I didn't want anyone unless it was someone God had for me. I was still learning about the things of God, and prayer was still very new to me. I wasn't exactly sure how to do this, but I felt like I needed to ask God if He had anyone for me. I asked God for a wife. I merely said:

"God, if you have someone for me, I'd like to be married again, but if you don't, I'll just serve you alone. I don't want anyone if it isn't from you."

I had no idea if scripturally or theologically I was doing it correct or not, but I really didn't give it a thought. I merely thought that I could talk to God and, if He wanted to, God could talk to me. (Childlike faith…I still love it.)

I don't know why this happened, but as soon as I prayed that prayer I began to cry, and I eventually cried myself to sleep. It was a very strange feeling, but a good feeling.

About 3:00 a.m. I opened my eyes wide awake, my mind clear and alert and I began to hear an inner voice speaking over and over again the same thing: Pam Skelton, Pam Skelton, Pam Skelton, over and over and over again.

I knew who she was, but I didn't really know her. All I knew for sure was that I kept hearing her name over and over and over again. To me and my childlike faith I thought, wow, does God really have somebody for me and has He given me their name already.

I'm sharing all this with you because, no matter what your need, Jesus is the answer. I have experienced it time and time again. Whatever you need from God, just ask. If he wants you to have it, you'll have it. If He doesn't want you to have it, you don't want it anyway.

I was really excited about what just happened, but I also was concerned. What if that wasn't really God? Also, if it was God, what was I supposed to do now. Find her and ask her to marry me? (Just kidding.)

The next day and every day after that evening, my mind was continually replaying what I heard over and over and over again. I couldn't stop it. It was all I ever thought about. I was really getting excited, because, even though I didn't really know for sure how these things from God worked, I was beginning to think that maybe I really had heard directly from God.

One day shortly after this experience I mentioned to my secretary, Jean, a simple question, "Do you know Pam Skelton?" I still don't know why I asked her that question.

"Why do you ask?" was her quiet reply with a look in her eyes I didn't like.

"No reason," was my feeble reply.

I quickly retreated to my office, only to see Jean appear in my doorway. Now what have I done? Why did I mention it to her? I should have just kept this to myself.

I finally told her that I thought perhaps God gave me her name in the middle of the night. I asked Jean if she knew Pam and she said she did, and she was not married. So far, so good.

I began to try to find Pam but had no success. How God eventually did bring us together was a miracle. One day my secretary Jean received a call from Pam asking Jean if I was alright. Pam shared with Jean that she kept hearing my name over and over again and thought that perhaps there was something she should be praying for me. Wow!

Jean got her phone number and we had our first date on Valentine's Day. I believe we both knew God was joining us together for His glory. I am blessed to have a beautiful wife inside and out. We were married shortly after at Oral Roberts University and dedicated our marriage to the Lord.

I don't believe I could have ever imagined where God was going to take Pam and me in our marriage, but it has been an awesome time of experiencing the miracle working power of God. There is no way I can thank God enough for what He did for me, and the blessings I have experienced through His love.

I didn't understand this then, but I believe God places desires in us, and then just waits until we ask Him for what that desire is.

"If we ask anything in His Name He will do it."

(JOHN 14:14)

"This is the confidence that we have in Him, that if we ask anything in accordance with His will, He hears us. And if we know He hears us, whatever we ask, we know that we have the petitions that we have asked of Him."

(1 JOHN 5:14-15)

My friend, God is no respecter of persons. What He has done for one, He will do for all. Let the deep inner desire of your heart surface and ask God for what you have need. He loves to bless those who love Him so that they can:

"MAKE THE BEST OF THE REST"

6

JESUS WAS ABOUT TO CHANGE EVERYTHING

In just a fairly short period of time I was about to find out that once Jesus comes into your life, everything begins to change. It was amazing. I knew that everything in my life was beginning to change, but I wasn't sure what it was changing to.

All I know for sure was that the more I read the word of God and prayed, the more I felt God had something for me to do, but I had no idea what it was. Nothing that I was currently doing seemed to hold my interest. As a matter of fact, the only thing that seemed to have any appeal to me was the word of God and prayer.

Eventually I sold the two businesses, and began to seek God for direction. I had heard that I should keep a prayer journal and record what I thought God was speaking to me.

I encourage you to be sure you have a prayer journal. If you have one, you know how important it is. If you don't have one, you are missing one of the most valuable assets available to you to record your past, present and future.

Because of the great advice I was given in the beginning of my walk with Jesus, I began keeping a daily prayer journal. It has been amazing. After almost forty years with Jesus, I have every prayer journal from the very beginning. It has been awesome to see where Jesus has brought me from.

Jesus had become real to me, and I pray that if this hasn't happened to you, it will. Once this happens it will begin to change your entire world. There begins to become a hunger and thirst for the things of God. The old ways of the world are not appealing any longer.

There is a great example of this in the Bible with Saul of Tarsus. He was a Pharisee and a member of the Sanhedrin, the religious organization of the Jews who ruled the Jewish people. He persecuted Christians wherever he went, and he was an accomplice in the death of the apostle Stephen when he was stoned to death.

By all accounts we read in the word of God, Saul was a very mean man, capable of brutal conduct including consenting to murder. He had received a letter of authority from the ruling Jewish Pharisees to travel to Damascus and take as prisoners every person he could find who was a believer in Jesus as the Son of God. Not really the type of guy you would want to hang out with.

This is the scene as he was traveling on the road to Damascus when he was intercepted by Jesus. Saul's story is fascinating proving that God will use whoever He wants, and whoever God wants to use will be changed forever by His Son Jesus.

Here is an overview of the account of Saul's trip to Damascus when Jesus first appeared to him:

"Saul, Saul, why are you persecuting Me? ... I am Jesus, whom you are persecuting. It is hard for you to kick against the goads ... Arise and go into the city, and you will be told what you must do."

(ACTS 9:4-6)

Paul had encountered a sudden light on his trip to Damascus that knocked him to the ground and took away for the moment his eyesight. Apparently, God wanted to get his attention, and this is the way He chose to do it.

I believe God loves us so much, and has a plan for our life, that He will do anything to get our attention so that we can pursue the destiny He has for us.

I know this was the case for Saul, and I believe the same is true for you and me.

I know Jesus was taking all of my earthly, worldly desires away when He came into my heart, and I believe He'll do the same with you. We can fight it and we can ignore it, but the only way we will ultimately be fulfilled in life is when we are pursuing His plan and purpose.

Maybe you are in a situation with the Lord right now, trying to hear clearly what His will is for your next season. Don't stop pressing in to hear from Him until you actually do. He will not withhold from you what He desires for you to know.

In my case it was a wonderful rewarding time, and an extremely frustrating time with the Lord. I can still remember vividly going to the Wabash River that flows through Lafayette, Indiana. There is a park that separates Lafayette from West Lafayette, and I would go there each morning and sit at a park bench talking to God.

This was such a new experience for me. Sometimes I would find myself talking to God, (I hoped), and sometimes I would start watching the birds fly by or the squirrels playing. It was an enjoyable distraction, but I was on a mission. I only had so much time to hear from God, and I was ready to hear. The only problem was, I didn't really know how to hear from God.

I still don't know exactly how this works, but even to this day after almost forty years in ministry, I'm still not sure exactly how it works. Sometimes when I go to pray and hear from God through His precious Holy Spirit, I begin to hear immediately…I like that! Sometimes I do the exact same thing on other days, and it appears I don't hear anything. What I do know for sure is this, when God is ready to show me what He wants me to know, He does.

As I would continue to pray, either at the river or somewhere else, I would always record in my prayer journal what I thought I heard at that moment. Then later I would read what I had recorded to determine if I really thought that it was from God.

Even though I often felt frustrated that I wasn't hearing clearly from God, I knew the problem was with me and not

God. Somehow, I did have faith to believe that God would show me what He wanted me to do with the rest of my life.

I would tell God that I would do whatever He wanted me to do. By now I had no interest in pursuing the business I had. I wanted to serve God, but I didn't know what that meant. My wife saw my continual frustration, and always encouraged me to keep praying, that God would eventually show me His direction.

I continually told God I would do whatever He had for me, that I just wanted to fulfill His plan and purpose for my life. I had read just enough scripture to believe that there was a plan for my life, and God knew what it was.

It seemed as though I went through this routine for an eternity, but it was really just a few short months. I think God may have been waiting for me to continually pour out my heart that I would do whatever He showed me to do, realizing that I just might not want to do what He wanted me to do.

After a few months of praying I began to hear in my spirit man the same thing. It was very short, and very simple:

"Go to Tulsa and you'll find the meaning for your life."

Okay, I'm thinking I have finally heard from God. I wasn't too sure I was too excited about Tulsa, but I was supercharged to think I had heard from God and that He did have an assignment for me. Now I'm just waiting to write the next part of what He is going to show me.

I heard nothing else. It was as if the communication ended. Must be a problem on my end, because I know God is getting ready to show me what I'll be doing in Tulsa.

That part never happened. I was frustrated. I began to hear the same thing continually, but nothing else.

"Go to Tulsa and you'll find the meaning for your life."

I began to share this with my wife because by now, I am hearing the same thing over and over again. Something is wrong. There must be more. I know I'm still new at praying and hearing from God, but I just know there has to be more.

As I continued to share this with my wife, I think I was secretly hoping that she would say we can't do that if we don't know what we are going to do. Surprise!

She responded that if that's where I think God wants us to go…let's go!

I wasn't prepared for that. Now what do I do. Being led by the word of God and the leading of the Holy Spirit was new to me. I saw how it worked when I asked God for a wife, but this was a little different. How do you just move from Indiana to Tulsa not really knowing what the overall plan is?

None of this made much sense to me. I could not seemingly wrap my mind of understanding around this move to Tulsa. I hadn't yet really understood one of God's powerful scriptures regarding understanding:

"Trust in the Lord with all your heart, and lean not to your own understanding. In all your ways acknowledge Him, and He shall direct your paths."

(PROVERBS 3:5-6)

There are times when we are serving the Lord when there will be difficult decisions to make. The right decision is always to follow the leading of God's Holy Spirit, regardless of the apparent cost.

When Pam and I married we each had three children. I was hoping we were putting together the Brady Bunch. I think the only thing that resembled the Brady Bunch was the number six...not much else.

My wife and I continued to pray to be absolutely sure we were both in agreement that it was God's will through the leading of His precious Holy Spirit that we were to relocate to Tulsa and there I would find the meaning for my life.

The agreement was solid and fortified between us.

Now for the more difficult part. It was time to tell our children and our families that God's plan was for us to relocate to Tulsa. It was at first a little difficult, but eventually everyone was on the same page (I think!). Our parents and families wished us well, but somehow, I think there were a few wondering if we were really doing the right thing. All were extremely supportive.

We knew Pam's children would all be with us, and I had hoped all mine would, but I knew that my daughter would probably stay with her mother. My boys initially gave an indication they would go with us, but that later changed. They also were going to stay with their mother.

I don't know what I was hoping for exactly, but I know it wasn't that. I really think that somewhere in my mind I saw us all riding off into the sunset to Tulsa living happily ever after. A great dream that never materialized.

Now I had somewhat of a dilemma. I told God I would go. I felt He was leading me to go, but I did not want to leave my children behind. That didn't make sense to me, and it still doesn't, but I finally settled the issue with much heartache. God wanted me in Tulsa. The issue was settled if I wanted to obey God.

I know there are some who would say God would never separate you from your children like that. Maybe they are right, but to this day, I believe I did what God asked me to do. The drive to Tulsa with my wife was one of the most difficult experiences of my life. I am not ashamed to say I cried most of the way, and even though I felt my heart was breaking, I knew that God would eventually heal me and use me for His glory to heal others.

God did give me a word during this period, and it really helped me when the enemy would come and tell me what a terrible father I was. How could any father leave his children like you did?

God's word for me:

> *"If you'll do what I've called you to do,*
> *I'll take care of your children."*

Maybe you have faced a similar type of situation in your life, or maybe you're facing one now. I know from my personal experiences, the most important thing in all our lives must be to follow the leading of the Holy Spirit. God knows exactly what He is doing. He knows the master plan, we don't. We only know the part that He decides to share with us for the moment.

I did watch as the Lord did take care of my children. I'm still not sure they understood everything that was happening at the time, but I knew they loved me and I loved them. That love has just grown deeper over the years. They are doing well, and I'm very proud of them.

I must say that Tulsa was quite an adventure and experience for me…actually, for all of us. I really wasn't sure what was coming next, but I had made a decision that God knew what He wanted me to do, and if I continued to follow him, He would lead me, guide me, and provide.

God was truly about to change everything in my life. All of my preconceived ideas were about to go by the wayside. God was making it quite simple for me; He would lead, and I would follow. If I got off on the wrong direction, He would immediately correct me, and I was corrected a lot. It seemed like it was a time of great victory, great defeat, abundance, lack, faith, fear, doubt and unbelief all mixed into one depending on the day.

You probably know what I'm talking about. One moment you think you're doing exactly what you feel the Lord showing you, only to find out later, that really wasn't His plan. That thing you pursued was your plan.

Don't let go of what you feel the Lord has shown you through His word and the leading of the Holy Spirit. If you don't give up, you'll eventually make it. And when you do make it, you'll look back and realize the journey was well worth the effort. God is always with us. If we continue to follow His leading, we will eventually reach the point where we are truly ready to:

"MAKE THE BEST OF THE REST"

7

FINDING THE MEANING FOR YOUR LIFE

Far too many people go through life without really finding the meaning for their life. By that I mean what is God's plan and purpose for our lives. God knows each of us intimately, and for each of us there is a specific plan and purpose for our life on this earth.

It has been my experience that many people either don't believe this, or have never spent time with God to ask what He would like for them to pursue. I do believe there is another group. This group has heard from God His plan for their lives, but they are going to ignore it and act like they didn't hear. Possibly because they don't want to do it, or possibly because they don't know how to do it.

During my initial period of time in Tulsa, I began to hear what I thought might be the word of God for me in my spirit, but it was something I couldn't imagine. As the old saying goes, "I couldn't wrap my mind around it."

My wife and I had started attending a new church in Tulsa, Victory Christian Center. The Pastors, Billy Joe and Sharon Daugherty, were young and I really liked the messages. Each one seemed to be exactly what I needed to hear. I always came away from the service feeling good about myself, uplifted and joyful.

I didn't realize this at the time, but through the messages at Victory, God was healing my heart and teaching me about righteousness, showing me that not only has God forgiven me through His Son, but that He has also forgotten all the terrible things I once did. And, not only did I learn He had forgiven me, I also learned that He even forgot all of my past sins. Wow!

We had only been attending a few services when my life was dramatically changed. I had never met Pastor Daugherty, but somehow, I had a confidence in him that he heard from God.

I was really struggling with trying to figure out what I was going to do with the rest of my life. The biggest problem I had was that I was trying to figure out the plan instead of letting God show me the plan.

Actually, God was continually trying to show me, but I just couldn't believe it could be God, so I did the foolish thing of just ignoring what I was hearing. I know that doesn't even make sense, but it's true. Who am I to do that?

What I had been feeling in my spirit was that perhaps God wanted me in some type of full-time ministry. I couldn't really envision it. As I said earlier, it just didn't make sense that God could use me.

I had given my life to Jesus as described earlier in the pastor's office of a denominational church. It was a wonderful evangelistic church, and they really helped a lot of people in the community. They did, however, have a policy in their denomination at that time that no one who had ever been divorced could be ordained into full time ministry.

No problem for me. I knew what my past was like. God may have forgiven me and forgotten my past, but I still remembered.

At Victory Christian Center in Tulsa, I heard a message that through God's love, acceptance and forgiveness, His original plan for our lives had never changed. I heard that He was a God of restoration.

Now I was somewhat conflicted. I felt God could not use me, but the messages I heard contradicted what I felt. I wanted to serve God, but I didn't feel worthy. I was still trying to understand righteousness. It was at best a challenging time for me.

Finally, I asked God to do something for me. I was young in the Lord, and in my simple-like, child-like faith, I made the following request to God:

"Lord, if You are really calling me into full-time ministry, please have Pastor Billy Joe call me up in front of the entire congregation and I will know it is You calling Me."

Only a few days after praying that prayer, I was sitting in a meeting prior to a Wednesday evening service. My father and mother-in-law had just sent me a pair of new shoes, and I was wearing them for the first time. As I sat in the meeting and adjusted the buckle on one of the shoes, it broke, and immediately I heard this:

"Tonight, Pastor Billy Joe will call you up
in front of the congregation."

I really didn't understand what I was hearing, even though it was quite clear. Being led by the Holy Spirit and hearing from the Holy Spirit was still something rather new to me. It was as if I couldn't believe what I believed I was hearing.

As a matter of fact, I totally dismissed what I heard, and after the meeting I went into the Wednesday night service to have an awesome encounter with my God.

The service started as usual with up-beat contemporary worship. It was inspiring as always. There is nothing to compare with being in a room full of people who love Jesus and express that love through their worship of Him.

After probably thirty minutes of worship, Pastor Billy Joe came forward and transitioned the service from worship to the next item on the agenda before he received the offering and shared the message.

He announced that we would be praying for Ulf Ekman, a young man who had just graduated from Rhema Bible Training Center, in Broken Arrow, Oklahoma. Ulf would be returning to Uppsala, Sweden to start a church.

Pastor Billy Joe called Ulf up in front of the congregation and walked around to the side of Ulf as if he were getting ready to pray for him. He first looked toward Ulf, then he looked back toward the congregation and just stared. Then he said the following words that immediately penetrated my spirit:

"Brother, you have the love of Jesus all over you.
You come up here and pray for Ulf."

I was in the last row of the congregation…frozen! I was not moving. Was he calling me? He doesn't even know me. I just stood there.

It was as if a sea of people in front of me began to part, and there was Pastor Billy Joe, looking directly at me and I was looking directly at him. I placed my hands and fingers inward toward my chest indicating with my lips, but no volume: "Me?"

I will never forget that night or his response:

"Yes. You!"

I had never prayed for anyone before in a public setting. I have no idea what words came through me, but I do know Pastor Ulf Ekman eventually had an outstanding church in Sweden reaching many people with the love of Jesus.

On the way back to my seat in the congregation I heard the Holy Spirit of God speak the following into my spirit:

"I did what you asked Me to do, now will you
do what I have called you to do?"

When I replay that evening over and over again, I feel the same emotions overtake me. God is a God of love, and His unconditional love toward us all is almost beyond description. He cares about every aspect of our lives.

That evening God confirmed to me what He had already placed in my heart, and he is no respecter of persons. What He has done for me, he will also do in some form or another for you. You see, I already knew He was calling me, but it was so difficult for me to see myself the way He saw me.

No matter where you are at the present time in your walk with the Lord, He desires to use you. He wants to heal your heart, He wants to restore your life, and He wants to use your testimony to reach out and help others find the manifestation of God's endless love through His Son Jesus.

Once the decision was made by me that God was calling me, the doors of opportunity began to open. I didn't open them, God did.

If you know what God has called you to do with your life, be sure to write it down and let him expand it for you when He is ready. It is God who opens the doors for us to walk through when the time is right. Don't rush His timing, and don't fall behind when His opportunities are presented.

There is nothing more rewarding than knowing that during your time on this earth there is a plan and a purpose for you to give your life for. It makes every day a new day to realize, that no matter what you're going through today, or tomorrow, good, bad or ugly…there is a master plan for your life. A race for you to run for God's glory.

No matter how many times you happen to miss the mark, make a mistake, or do something and just shake your head and wonder why you did it, just learn from it.

Realize that every experience you have will just help you to:

"MAKE THE BEST OF THE REST"

8

FAITH PLEASES GOD

I felt God had answered my prayer of asking Him to do something to assure me that I was actually hearing from Him. Now what do I do?

My basic nature would be to always have a plan to do something, and the one, two, three step approach to how to implement the plan and accomplish the goal.

It wasn't exactly rocket science, but I understood the principle of setting a goal and then pursuing it.

I was in for a total make over adjustment in my life, and I wasn't at all aware of how frustrating and rewarding the experience was going to be. I thank God that I now had a wife alongside me who truly understood the message of faith that I was about to encounter and struggle with. Jesus and my wife really helped me to understand the message of faith. As I look back on those days now, I realize how fortunate I was to have a wife who had the patience to endure with me as I entered into the walk of faith.

The word of God in Proverbs 3:5-6 that I have shared in a previous chapter states specifically the we should "not lean to our own understanding." That was very hard for me. As a matter of fact, it is even still hard for me. I like to understand.

I realized that my faith level to serve God, and, accomplish His plan for my life was not where it needed to be. I was still learning the word of God, still trying to learn how to get my mind renewed and keep it renewed. It seemed like a never-ending process, and it was and still is.

Resources were very tight during this period of time, and I was learning to walk by faith, and to live by faith. I must admit I wasn't too sure I liked this new venture. I'll give you an example.

One day Pam was scheduled to play tennis against a young girl who was a member of the Victory Christian Center tennis team. Pam and I had played quite a bit of tennis, and Pam was becoming quite good and competitive.

It was an outreach where the staff of Victory Christian School played against the school tennis team. I needed to take Pam over early to warm up for the event, and I knew we were about out of gas in our only car, and out of money.

During this period of my life, it seemed I was always out of money. Pam was working at the church in the Christian school and I was working a secular job in an employment agency. Financially it was extremely difficult.

I realize God was using this time in my life for my faith to expand and trust Him for everything. A totally new experience for me. How about you? You have had, and perhaps are even now having opportunities where you really need to release your faith in God for your basic needs.

At the time it was very difficult, but without those times, I don't think I would have been prepared to pursue some of the adventures God has had for me. To follow God, it takes obedience and faith to do what He shows us to do.

As I drove Pam to the tennis courts, I knew the gas gauge was moving very close to empty. I was learning to trust God, and do whatever He showed me to do, realizing He will take care of my every need. Even with that said, it was still very difficult for me to fight off my constant attempt to understand why this faith walk seemed so difficult. Again, I didn't realize I was being trained to walk by faith and not be moved by what I saw.

As I pulled into the parking area at the tennis courts and parked the car, a staff member at Victory came over and greeted me. He said he had been praying this morning, and the Lord instructed him to give me twenty dollars.

Needless to say, I was so excited, but part of me felt a little conflicted. God, I'm learning Your word. I'm trying to do what You tell me to do, however, it seems as though I can't even reach into my pocket and pull out enough money to put gas in my car without it being a miracle from You.

I can honestly say that during that period of time in my life, I didn't want to have to pray everything in. I just wanted things already without prayer. I wanted to know I had enough money for gas, enough money for food, etc., etc., etc. I think, I was complaining to God that I wasn't all that excited about His system of faith.

The complaining did me no good, but I found something that did...reading and meditating the word continually. My faith began to grow as I would read and study the word of God. It was amazing. The more word I read, the more word I memorized, the more my faith appeared to grow.

Perhaps you know that same feeling. I'm ready to serve you God, but don't know yet how I can do what I'm supposed to do if I don't have the finances. How do I pay the bills, take care of my family, save money and still do all the things you seem to be placing in my heart?

Yes, Lord, I want to serve You, and yes Lord, I want to do whatever you have for me to do, but how do I do it when I don't seem to have the financial ability to make it happen? Somehow it just didn't make sense to me.

God wanted me to learn how to develop my faith so that I would be able to follow Him wherever He would lead me, and I can assure you, He is doing the same thing with you. He wants to know that our faith is so strong that we will follow Him wherever He leads.

It is a very valuable lesson that we must learn, and the only way we truly learn it, in my opinion, is through trial and error. Sometimes we do it right and sometimes we do it wrong, but we must learn the lesson of walking by faith.

"We walk by faith and not by sight."

(2 CORINTHIANS 5:7)

At this point in my life, I wanted to serve God and hear clearly what He wanted me to do with my life, but when I would begin to hear something, I would immediately begin to try to understand how I could do it. I would try to figure everything out. I hadn't yet learned that if God was going to speak to me by His Spirit, He would also show me how to do what He was showing me to do by His Spirit. For me, this was a very difficult learning curve. How about you?

One thing I know for sure, and that is that at this time in my life, I did not have the revelation of two scriptures that would eventually change my life. There are many scriptures that have been instrumental in changing my life, but these two are two of the most foundational for me:

"I can do all things through Christ who strengthens Me."

(PHILIPPIANS 4:13)

"My God shall supply all of my needs according to His riches in heaven."

(PHILIPPIANS 4:19)

For some reason these two scriptures just seemed to bear witness in my spirit and in my mind, that whatever God wanted me to do, I could do. I believed that God would never ask me to do something if He didn't think I could do it.

God is concerned about meeting all of your needs, and sometimes we can have our eyes too fixed on our needs instead of focusing our attention on what God is asking us to do.

This calls to my remembrance something that happened during this period of time in my life when we first had arrived in Tulsa. Our church, Victory, was temporarily meeting in a tent in the parking lot of the church. The growth was happening so fast the pastor thought that was the direction to take for a period of time.

During one of the Sunday services, the pastor asked for a show of hands at the end of the service for those who had financial needs. Well, I was still deeply in debt, so I raised my hand.

He then instructed everyone who had raised their hands to come to the altar. This is all still fairly new to me, but reluctantly I went. After praying for everyone at the altar, he instructed the ushers to hand each of us at the altar an offering bucket, and he instructed the congregation to come forward as they felt led and bless those of us at the altar.

Well, I can tell you, I was really embarrassed. It wasn't so much that I didn't have money, it was the debt that I didn't know how to take care of. Even though I was deeply in debt, I did have some money. I'm sure it was just my pride, but I felt very awkward being at the altar with a bucket.

It seemed like I was at the altar for an eternity, but it was probably just a few minutes, someone came by and dropped a twenty-dollar bill in my bucket. As I started to return to my seat in the congregation, I heard a lady with an offering bucket standing near me explaining to someone that she didn't have many groceries.

At that moment, I didn't have any cash on me, but I had the twenty dollars in my offering bucket. I quickly took the twenty and placed it in her bucket and returned to my seat.

Could we have used the twenty? Yes, and many, many more multiplied over, but in my spirit, I felt I was to give the twenty to the lady.

The incident I just described happened almost thirty-seven years ago, but it is still as fresh in my mind as the day it happened. The feeling of compassion that came over me as I gave her the twenty penetrated my heart. There was no thought about my need, but only wishing I could do more to meet her need. I firmly believe that was a moment of God testing me.

God is desiring to have us follow Him with total trust and confidence in Him, knowing that He will take care of all our needs. In the meantime, as we journey on with Him, He wants us to do everything He shows us to do in meeting the needs of others.

I believe with all of my heart that when our focus is totally upon meeting the needs of others, we have God's attention. Our natural response many times can be, what about me? What about my needs?

If we are truly going to serve God, our concern will never be about our needs. Our total concern is meeting the needs of others as the Holy Spirit directs, and realizing that whatever we need to meet those needs, God will supply.

What are your needs today? You serve a God who cares deeply about meeting all your needs. Let Him know what you have need of, and thank Him for meeting those needs, then move on by faith and the leading of the Holy Spirit to help others. There is no greater thrill on earth that helping other people who are in need.

Just remember that we are following our faith in God in all that we do. We have our focus on our God knowing that He will supply our every need, and that through Him we truly can do all things. It is through our faith in God that allows us to follow Him, and not be moved by understanding.

As I reflect back on that experience in the tent service, I realize that I wasn't really thinking about walking or living by faith. The lady had a need, and I was able to help her, even though I'm sure the twenty dollars didn't go very far.

At that time there was no real understanding of faith, no understanding of planting seed. It was just a situation where a lady had a need and I was in the area with the ability to do something.

We continued to attend Victory Christian Center church, and we continued to hear messages about living a life of faith in serving a God who loved us. It was an exciting time as the church was continually growing.

I was working as a manager of an employment service in Tulsa, trying to be successful in supporting my family in Lafayette and my family in Tulsa. It wasn't going well. Financially it was a very difficult time, and there were many times I just wanted to give up on the faith message. It seemed to me like I was getting further and further behind.

When I would spend time praying, it was always as if I would hear in my spirit that I just needed to continue to press on. While I did press on, it was extremely frustrating, because nothing seemed to change financially.

God wants our faith in Him to be strong, enabling us to follow Him wherever He leads us.

I must admit that at this time in my life I did not have a revelation of the truth regarding the faith message. I was hearing it, but I didn't feel I was experiencing it. There were many times I just wanted to give up and pursue something else, but then I would just begin to laugh at myself, because I was entertaining pursuing something else, and I didn't even know what I was now pursuing.

In time the following two scriptures became real to me:

"Now faith is the substance of things hoped for, the evidence of things not seen."

(HEBREWS 11:1)

"But without faith it is impossible to please God, for he who comes to God must believe that He is a rewarder of those who diligently seek Him."

(HEBREWS 11:6)

It took me quite a while, but I eventually realized that I wasn't seeking God because I loved Him or wanted to serve Him. I was seeking Him because I believed He could bless my finances so that all my needs would be met.

I hope this makes sense to you, but I believe there were many times in my life when I just wanted to use God to get my needs met. There wasn't this overwhelming desire to give Him first place in my life. It was more like going to the banker and getting the money you needed to go on with your life.

I have had this experience with many people in my years of ministry. They knew God could meet their financial needs, and they were asking Him to do so, but they really weren't that interested in serving God.

To fulfill our God given destiny on earth, I believe it takes total faith in God to believe He can do all things through us if we will just yield our life to Him. He knows the plan, and He will supply all the need.

During this time period I believe God was watching me, testing me, to see if I would really pursue Him. There were many times when I seemed to fail the test, but God loves us so much, He is always willing to give us another chance, another test.

The messages at Victory through the pastor and almost all of the guest speakers during that era all seemed to center on the importance of faith, and I began to realize that I was not where I needed to be in my walk of faith with God.

Maybe you are in a similar situation. You know God has much more for you, but you just don't feel prepared and ready. My recommendation would be for you to do exactly what I did. I believe the Lord began to show me what to do, but it didn't make any sense to me.

As I look back now, I realize how important this decision was to prepare me for the future God had. He knows how to prepare us so that we can:

"MAKE THE BEST OF THE REST"

9

VICTORY BIBLE INSTITUTE MAKES NO SENSE

Our church in Tulsa had really been promoting the Bible school it had, Victory Bible Institute, and I did have a few thoughts about attending, but it didn't make any sense to me. One day Pam said that maybe I should pray about attending.

I brushed off her comment, not really remembering what I said, but I probably told her I didn't have time. At this time, I was forty-one years old, and going to Bible school for a year made no sense to me, however, the thought that was in my spirit of possibly attending the school never left me.

I can assure you that God, through His precious Holy Spirit, will always show you what He has for the next season of your life. He will probably not show you everything, but He will show you enough to get you started. God will never withhold from you what He desires for you to know.

Be sure to take what you think you may be hearing in your spirit, and record it in your prayer journal. This will build your faith and eventually become your spiritual road map. As I shared earlier, I have all my prayer journals from 1980 until the present, and they are a tremendous faith builder in addition to being my spiritual road map.

Pam and I began to discuss the possibility of my attending Victory Bible Institute full time. I use the following expression quite a bit, but it is so true: I just couldn't seem to wrap my mind around it, but in my spirit, I believed it was the right thing to do.

I spoke to the person who owned the employment office where I worked, and they gave me the okay to work part time. I would go to Bible school in the morning and work at the office in the afternoon. So far, so good.

During this period Pam had taken a job as the Administrative Assistant to the Director of Victory Christian School, so all was beginning to fall into place. I was still a little reluctant to go to Bible school at my age in addition to knowing the possibility of my income dropping by only working part time.

I share these stories of my life with you, because I believe we all have similar stories and experiences. You may not have a Bible school presenting itself, but there are opportunities that present themselves as we submit our will to God that we some-times are not sure about. Like me, we enter into them somewhat reluctant, releasing our faith in God and hoping we are making the right decision.

Having once started Bible school, I realized it was the right decision. I didn't realize how much I didn't know until I began to hear from the anointed teachers the truth about the word of God. It was an awesome experience.

A person doesn't have to go to Bible school to have their faith level strong enough to follow God wherever He may lead, but it certainly will not hurt. In this day and age of modern technology you can go to any one of many great Bible schools on-line in your home. I highly recommend it.

One thing is certain though regarding building our faith; it can only be done through the word of God and the leading of the Holy Spirit. We have the written word of God available to us, and we have the word of God brought to us by the Holy Spirit. It is imperative that we read the word of God and allow the Holy Spirit to reveal to us the current word God has for us.

"Faith comes by hearing and hearing by the word of God."

(ROMANS 10:17)

Jesus stated basically the same thing when the devil tried to attack Him during His forty days and nights in the wilderness:

"Man shall not live by bread alone, but by every word that proceeds from the mouth of God."

(MATTHEW 4:4)

Jesus, who was the Word of God made flesh, used the word of God against the devil releasing His faith in God's word. You and I must do the same. Without our faith in God's word, our faith is dead.

As a matter of fact, Jesus was quoting God's word from the Old Testament:

"And you shall remember that the Lord your God led you all the way these forty years in the wilderness, to humble you and test you, to know what was in your heart, whether you would keep his commandments or not. So, He humbled you, allowed you to hunger, and fed you with manna which you did not know, nor did your fathers know, that He might make you know that man shall not live by bread alone, but man shall live by every word that proceeds from the mouth of God."

(DEUTERONOMY 8:2-3)

The word of God is the foundation for our faith, and I also believe the word of God can mean the difference between life and death. It is in the continual hearing of the word of God that our faith grows.

With these thoughts in mind that I just shared with you, I now share some of my most difficult moments in Victory Bible Institute. I hope and pray it can help you in areas where you are going through perhaps similar frustration.

I was well into the year learning much and having my faith grow with each of the classes, but there was a constant challenge in my mind. The financial situation was growing worse each day, and I finally decided to make an appointment to see the Director of the Bible School. I had discussed it with my wife, and while she thought I should stay in school, she said she would back me in whatever I decided to do.

When I sat down with the Director and told him the story of my finances, he shared with me something I have never forgotten.

He said he didn't really know the answer regarding the financial situation, but what he did share changed my life. He said, "Bill, it has to reach the point in your life when Jesus is more real to you than anything. More real to you than any situation. More real to you than your wife or anything you are facing."

I thought for a moment about what he said, and then I responded: "He's not that real to me. I need to drop out of VBI."

I walked out of his office, got in my car, and began to just drive with no particular destination. Tears began to flood down my cheeks as I asked God to forgive me for what I said, but I also told God that what I said was true. I was not where I should be spiritually.

Do you remember reading in Chapter 2 when I stated that I was about to make a bad situation worse? Well, I was about to do it again. I was walking out of the place where God had placed me, and it was about to become a very bumpy ride.

I made the decision to interview at Mc Donald's for a management position. My background had been in management in the food industry, so I thought I might as well go back and give it a try. At least I knew the salary would be decent.

I now know that I was walking directly into a trap the devil was setting. He was doing everything in his power to get my attention on the finances and away from what God had for me. I am sure the Holy Spirit was warning me, but I wasn't listening.

Even now as I look back, I can't believe I did it. I'm sure you may have some reflective moments also when you look back at decisions you made after you had received Jesus as your Lord and Savior and now wondered how you could have made the decision that you did.

Pam and I laugh about it now, but there was nothing funny about the situation at the time. Nothing!

Some days I would work the day shift and get off around 5 or 6 p.m. Other days I might go in at 5 or 6 p.m. and work until 1 or 2 a.m. Then again on other days I might go to work at 3 or 4 a.m. and work until noon or later. It was horrible. I couldn't tell most of the time if I was coming or going. Very difficult for me, my wife and the family.

I finally realized I had made a mistake, but I didn't know exactly what to do about it. One day I had just stepped into the shower after working a shift. I wasn't really praying or thinking much of anything, but I heard what I believed was a strong word from the Lord:

> *"You must return to VBI immediately or you'll miss the timing I have for your life."*

Great. Now I have to go tell my wife I have missed God's plan for my life. I have to tell her that this horrible schedule I have put us through these last two months was a mistake on my part. On top of telling her I had made a mistake and I needed to return to Bible school immediately, I knew that she had never wanted me to leave Bible school in the first place.

I went out to tell her what I heard, wondering how she would respond. I was amazed at what she said. She had heard the exact same word that I had. We were in total agreement that I should go back to Bible school immediately.

During that time away from Bible school, I really attempted to draw close to Jesus. I wanted that relationship the VBI Director talked about. In the natural realm it was a difficult time working at Mc Donald's, but in the realm of the spirit, it was an awesome time. I can honestly say that Jesus really became real to me during that period. Truly God will use all things for good.

Perhaps at this very moment you are going the wrong way, and you know it. Don't keep moving in the wrong direction. Ask God to show you what to do. He loves you, and He will show you the direction to take. Take it!

When I left VBI it was because of our financial situation. When I returned to VBI, the financial situation was still bad, however, my faith in Jesus was strong. I knew that if I didn't give up, He would bring us through. Sure enough, He did.

Victory Bible Institute was one of the things that truly changed my life. I had complicated my life by leaving, but now I was back. Because I had missed one session, I now had to attend the morning classes and the evening classes.

Now I was paying the price for my mistake, but it was alright...I was learning. I was learning how to live the word of

God, how to walk by faith and not by sight, and how to hear the still small inner voice of the Holy Spirit. It was awesome.

If you will stay on the path that God has for your life, the blessings will eventually overtake you. I began to see that happen. Little by little I began to see the hand of God moving in many areas of my life. Truly, if we will obey the voice of God, His blessing will come upon us.

> *"And all these blessings shall come upon you and overtake you, because you obey the voice of the Lord your God."*
>
> (DEUTERONOMY 28:2)

It is really important to do everything in your power to be in the center of God's will and His timing. I came very close to missing both. I believe with all my heart that God loves us so much, that He will do everything He can to get our attention and get us on the right path. He got mine in the shower and I'm so glad He did.

Once I returned to VBI the quality of my life really improved. The classes at Bible school were awesome, the messages Pastor Billy Joe preached really impacted my life, and I was excited about the future, but also a little apprehensive.

What was I going to do after Bible school? I really didn't have a long-range vision. I just knew that I was to go to Bible school. Sometimes we just need to concentrate on what God tells us to do for the present, realizing He has the master plan for the future. Regardless, I was still beginning to wonder where I was going to go and what was God going to have me do.

One day as I was sitting in one of our church services at the Mabee Center in Tulsa, Oklahoma, listening to Pastor Billy Joe preach, I heard this in my spirit:

"You are going to go on staff at Victory Christian Center."

I felt in my spirit I was given the name of the person who would be instrumental in bringing me on staff, however I quickly discounted everything I heard because Pastor Daugherty announced this person was leaving his staff position at Victory and moving to another state. My thought: I must not have heard from God.

A word of encouragement to you; whatever you think you hear from the Lord, even if you're not sure it is from the Lord, write it in your prayer journal. You will be amazed over the years and it will build your faith.

About two months later Pastor Daugherty announced the individual who I thought I heard would be instrumental in my joining the staff at Victory was returning to become the Director of Victory Bible Institute.

When I heard the announcement, I didn't even think about the word I had heard about two months earlier. No kidding, the fact that this person was returning did not bring back to my remembrance what I thought I heard.

The following Sunday this individual was back in Tulsa at the Mabee Center where Victory was holding services. There is a big escalator at the entrance, and as I was coming down, I saw him walking through the foyer. He looked up at me and shouted: "Mickler, I need to talk with you right away. Come see me Monday."

Immediately, I heard in my spirit the same words I heard two months earlier:

"You are going to go on staff at Victory Christian Center."

I was excited, but I was still somewhat apprehensive. Hearing clearly from the Holy Spirit is a lifetime experience of learning. After almost forty years of attempting to follow the Holy Spirit, I still find the trial and error part to be true. No error on the part of the Holy Spirit. Only error on my part as to whether or not I was really tuned in to the leading of the Holy Spirit or just something I thought. A big difference!

Maybe you're facing situations in your life where you are trying to clearly determine if you are hearing from the Holy Spirit. All of us know what we hear. It is only with time and practice by spending time with the Holy Spirit, that we eventually begin to recognize His voice.

Over a period of time, it is possible to develop our faith to begin to recognize the inner voice of the Holy Spirt speaking into our spirit. I know this for certain, it is much easier for me to identify the voice of the Holy Spirit today than it was years ago.

It is really not much different than the example of meeting someone for the first time. You hear their voice, but if they called you on your cell after the first meeting, you may not recognize their voice.

When I first met my wife, I heard her voice for the first time. I may or may not have recognized her voice in a crowd after that first meeting, but after almost forty years of marriage, I can recognize her voice immediately. I must admit, I love to hear her voice.

That's the way it needs to be with the voice of the Holy Spirit. The more years we spend cultivating that relationship, the quicker we are to identify that voice. I believe one of the most important priorities in every person's life is to develop the ability to immediately recognize and embrace the leading of the Holy Spirit. This is the number one way we can determine God's truth and guidance for us.

I believe Jesus summed it up as follows:

"However, when He, the Spirit of truth has come, He will guide you into all truth. He will not speak on His own authority, but whatever He hears, He will speak and tell you of things to come. He will glorify Me, for He will take what is mine, and declare it to you. All things that the Father has are Mine. Therefore, I said that He will take of Mine and declare it to you."

(JOHN 16:13-15)

Think about that word from Jesus for just a moment. Actually, you need to take the importance of what Jesus said and meditate it the rest of your life. God wants to reveal to us what He wants us to know to prepare us, then when we begin to pursue what He has shown us, we release our faith that whatever we have need of, He will provide, just as everything Jesus had need of was provided.

So now I'm headed to a meeting with the new Director of Victory Bible Institute meditating on the word the Lord had given me about going on staff at Victory Christian Center. Needless to say, I was really excited. Having the Holy Spirit prepare you for what was to come, without revealing all the details, was still a fairly new experience for me, but I was really beginning to like it.

After some informal small talk, the Director of VBI moved quickly to the point of the meeting. He wasn't one to waste time. He asked me if I would take a position assisting him with overseeing the part time VBI night school while continuing on as a full-time day student. There would be small salary, and my tuition to VBI would be paid.

He also explained that VBI was starting a second-year program that would be an internship, and he would like me to be enrolled in addition to helping him oversee the entire program. My excitement was now off the chart. Not just the position and salary offered, but more than anything knowing I truly had the ability to hear from the Holy Spirit.

God wants us to have confidence in Him, that not only does He desire to speak to us, but He desires that we have the faith and confidence that we can hear from Him whenever He desires to speak. The key is, are we always willing to listen. All of us are guilty of sometimes becoming to busy to be continually listening for God's voice through the precious Holy Spirit.

I have often wondered what would have happened in my life if I hadn't returned to Bible school when the Holy Spirit spoke to me. What if I hadn't been listening? Would God have tried to reach me in a different manner? Would I have just drifted on with life missing God's plan?

I'm not sure what the answers would be to those questions, but one thing I am absolutely positive about, and that is that the most important thing in our lives regarding completing our God given assignment is to develop and maintain the ability to continually hear the voice of the Holy Spirit when He speaks.

I am not sharing the following to exalt me. No one stands in more amazement than me at what followed the meeting I had with the Director of VBI. I am forever grateful for the door the Lord had him open for me at Victory Christian Center.

From the beginning of my assignment I seemed to get more and more delegated responsibilities. I loved it. I was working in a rapidly growing ministry, had a position I really enjoyed, learning the word of God during the day in school, working afternoons in an office in the church, and overseeing and attending the part time evening school. It sure didn't leave much time for my wife or family, but I knew it was what God had for me for the season we were in.

After completing the first year of Bible school with my new position, I was placed in charge of putting together much of the format and curriculum for the second year internship program. I was really delegated quite a bit of authority and I liked it. I knew the basic vision, so it was somewhat easy to put together the format for the year. Dealing with the personalities of the various interns was not quite as easy as the formatting of the program.

The internship went by quickly, and soon I was offered the position as the Assistant Director of Victory Bible Institute. Wow! I would still wonder what would have happened if I hadn't listened to the Holy Spirit in my shower a year earlier.

After another year they made me the Director of Victory Bible Institute. I don't think I thought I was qualified, but if that's what God wants, I'm on board. It was an awesome experience. There were students coming from all over America and even from foreign countries. A very exciting time for my wife and me. She was at this time now working for the previous Director of VBI who had been promoted to be the Associate Pastor. She was really busy, but it was great that we were working in the ministry in different departments, but not yet together. Our desire was that someday we could work in the same area together.

Shortly after another year as the Bible school director I was given the additional responsibility of becoming the Director of Victory Fellowship of Ministries. I will never forget the way the announcement for that promotion took place.

There was a meeting of ministers on the sixtieth floor of the old City of Faith building, and Pastor Billy Joe was conducting the dinner meeting. My wife and I were working behind the scene, and the pastor was announcing the former Associate Pastor was leaving to pastor a church in Texas. He was a good man, and we were happy for him.

One of his responsibilities was to oversee Victory Fellowship of Ministries. It is an organization of Victory Christian Center that at the time had about seven hundred ministry members across the United States and the throughout the world.

Pastor Billy Joe thanked the previous Associate Pastor, had him share a few words, and then announced that the new Director of Victory Fellowship of Ministries would be Bill Mickler.

I was standing next to my wife when the announcement was made. She looked at me and said, "Why didn't you tell me?" I smiled and said, "You heard it when I did."

Working for a visionary pastor like Billy Joe Daugherty was one of the most awesome experiences of my life, and, it was one of the most interesting. You truly never knew what he was going to do, but you had confidence in him, that he was always going to do what he thought the Holy Spirit showed him.

I'll give you a great example of not knowing what to expect with Pastor Billy Joe that really helped prepare me for the future, even though at the time I only realized that if I was going to work with him and serve him, I would certainly have to be led by the Holy Spirit also.

I have numerous stories I could share regarding working for this man, but I'll try to limit it to just one. It took place at Christ Chapel on the campus of Oral Roberts University, and it was a classic Billy Joe Daugherty.

I'm not sure why we were meeting at Christ Chapel instead of the Mabee Center, but it was a Wednesday evening service. At that time communion was served each Wednesday immediately after praise and worship. Pastor Billy Joe would always share a short message and then we would all take communion.

At that time my wife and I were seated on the platform in the second row behind the pastor and his wife. As one of the Assistant Pastors I knew to be ready to take any direction the pastor gave or get him whatever he needed.

As we were all worshiping the Lord with about 2,000 people in attendance, the pastor leaned toward me in the row behind him. I realized he needed something, so I leaned forward, all of this taking place while we were singing praise songs to God.

He whispered, "Did Eula Mae call you today about doing communion?"

Eula Mae was a sweet, wonderful lady, and his secretary.

I was startled, because I had never done communion.

I tried to very calmly reply, "No."

He leaned back continuing to worship the Lord, and then again leaned back to me and asked, "Are you prepared to do communion?"

Now I think I was startled with an addition of anxiety, all while we are continuing to worship the Lord, as I leaned forward and whispered, "No."

He continued to worship the Lord, but in just a few seconds time, leaned back again and whispered, "How long does it take you to get prepared?"

I knew the answer he was expecting, and I gave it. I replied, "I'm prepared."

When I think back about this night now, I usually start laughing, but it was anything but humorous at the moment. I knew he wanted me to do the communion, so obviously he felt he had heard from the Holy Spirit.

I'm thinking that while he may have heard from the Holy Spirit, I seemed to be clueless. I was trying to remember exactly what we did at communion.

He leaned back one final time, again as we were worshipping the Lord and said,

"You take it out worship."

That meant that any second the worship would end with the instrumentation playing softly in the background as I went forward taking the microphone from the worship leader and sharing a brief message I didn't have as to the death and resurrection of Jesus. I truly thought to myself, "This is going to be interesting."

I was trying to remember exactly what to do, when I heard the worship leader end the last song, begin to walk toward us, and realized it was time for me to share. I still remember vividly what happened.

Again, this was my first time to share, and I had arrived totally unprepared. By the way, it was the last time I ever arrived unprepared.

As I took the microphone from our worship leader and walked slowly to the podium I softly, internally prayed, "Lord, please help me to share."

I remember briefly sharing about the importance of communion, and how much God loved us. I then shared how important it was to receive God's love.

I gave everyone an opportunity to do that and as I did, I remember feeling that the words were not coming from my head, but from my spirit.

My eyes were closed as I prayed for those who did not know Jesus, had never accepted Him as their Lord and Savior, or as a prodigal child drifted away from God, and shared that if I had described them, to raise their hand and I would pray for them.

I waited a few seconds, and then opened my eyes. Unbelievable! There were hands raised throughout the congregation. I was somewhat astounded. From there I'm not sure what else I shared regarding communion, but I do remember leading all those people to Jesus or back to Jesus.

As we transitioned out of communion I walked back to my seat, and I felt the Holy Spirit speak into my spirit, "That was not you who did that, but it was the power of My anointing." I have never forgotten that moment.

Shortly after this they placed me over Pastoral Care, Benevolence, and for a for a one-year period Victory World Mission Training Center. It came so fast that I really asked myself one day, "Do they really know what they are doing?"

I knew my past. I knew they didn't know all I had been through. I must admit I never felt myself qualified to do anything they were asking me to do. It was wonderful opportunities that were presenting themselves, but I always felt somewhat inadequate.

Over my years in ministry I have encountered many people who have felt inadequate. Call it a lack of confidence, or any other description, but I believe there are numerous people God wants to use who do not feel worthy to be used by Him. I certainly believe I was one of them.

Don't let your past hold you back from your future. Don't let your past define your future. You are destined by God to become whoever He says you are to become, and you are destined by God to accomplish for His glory whatever He says you are to accomplish for His glory. What you think has no bearing on what God thinks, but what God thinks should have total bearing on what you think.

Proverbs gives a glimpse at how important what we think really is:

"As a man thinks in his heart, so is he."

(PROVERBS 23:7)

As I reflect back on this period of time, it was as if God had opened the windows of heaven and poured out a tremendous blessing upon our lives. Pam was busy working for the Associate Pastor and Pastor Billy Joe on various projects, the children who were with us were doing well in school, and life was great.

During this period Pam had been asked by Pastor Billy Joe if she would help him with a project Oral Roberts wanted to launch. The vision Oral had was to start an organization for ministers, to be known as International Charismatic Bible Ministries, and Pam would be responsible to work alongside Pastor Billy Joe setting up the network of ministries and assisting with the organization of the first conference on the beautiful campus of Oral Roberts University.

I share some of our experiences to make the following important point. We were happy, content, and fulfilled. All was going well, but there was about to be a major change on the horizon.

For several years in Tulsa, my wife felt that someday we would return to Lafayette, Indiana and pastor a church. I had no intention of ever returning to Lafayette. That was the land of my past giants and I wanted no part of it.

As a matter of fact, my wife was at a Victory Fellowship of Ministries meeting one night playing the piano for worship. Pastor Billy Joe was sharing, and he had a word from the Lord that those in attendance would go out and pioneer ministry works for the Lord.

Pam came home excited that she felt we would be one of them. I promptly shared with her that we were staying at Victory with Pastor Billy Joe and Sharon until Jesus returned. Not much prayer or leading of the Holy Spirit in my response, but quite a bit of firmness in my voice. (Pam still remembers.)

Even though everything was really going well, I felt something was happening in my spirit. I wasn't sure what it was, but I felt like the Lord was getting ready to show me something. I was deeply involved in the things of the ministry, but I was feeling less and less attached. I couldn't understand it.

Finally, the Lord showed me the direction we were to take. We were to return to Lafayette and start a church. I felt everything inside me desire to do what God was showing me, but at the same time I felt everything inside me not wanting to leave Victory or Pastors Billy Joe and Sharon. It was a very interesting time.

Eventually I knew we had to give our notice and move on with the guidance of the Holy Spirit to fulfill God's plan for us. It was very, very emotional for me, but I knew it was God's will.

The last service we were in when we said goodbye and thanked God and Pastors Billy Joe and Sharon for the opportunity, I still remember what I said, "We are not leaving Victory; we are taking Victory to Lafayette."

Once the decision was made, the conflicted pressure I had been feeling was gone. Now I knew we had made the decision God had for us and we were free to:

"MAKE THE BEST OF THE REST"

10

DENY YOURSELF AND FOLLOW JESUS

It is amazing the emotions that you go through as you follow Jesus attempting to fulfill God's plan for your life. It was so difficult for me to leave Lafayette, Indiana and move to Tulsa. A very emotional experience.

Now I'm leaving Victory Christian Center in Tulsa, and, returning to Lafayette with another very emotional experience. Thank God for the peace and comfort that is always available through His precious Holy Spirit.

In situations like this I often think of the words of Jesus:

"If anyone desires to come after Me let him deny himself, and take up his cross and follow Me. For whoever desires to save his life will lose it, but whoever loses his life for My sake will find it. For what profit is it to a man if he gains the whole world and loses his own soul? Or what will a man give in exchange for his soul? For the Son of Man will come in the

*glory of His Father with His angels, and then He will
reward each according to his works."*

(MATTHEW 16:24-27)

Right up until the time when we actually left Tulsa, I was
continually praying and asking God if I was doing the right
thing. In response to that prayer, one day I received a letter that
had been sent from a lady in Lafayette, Indiana addressed to
Pastor Billy Joe Daugherty asking him if Victory would ever be
planting a church in Lafayette. Wow! Amazing!

To me that was the confirmation I needed. It really helped
me to focus on what God was speaking into my spirit. I must
admit, however, that I was still trying to find a way to not return
to Lafayette. I tried to tell my wife that perhaps we should start
the church in Indianapolis. I even made a trip back to see if
there was a site that God had for us there.

I realized as I was looking around Indianapolis that this
wasn't the destination God had for us. God was calling us to
Lafayette, a place that I had told God I would not return to. Be
careful what you are telling God you aren't going to do. As a
matter of fact, if you really want to get God's attention, just
begin to tell Him what you aren't open to do.

That reminds me of another thing I told God I wasn't going
to do. Pam's mom and dad had shared with us that we could live
with them until we started the church. I said no. I didn't want
to live with anyone.

By now you can probably guess where we lived when we
first came back to Lafayette. That's right, with Pam's mom and

dad. I must say it was an awesome and wonderful time. They were so kind, gracious and hospitable. It was a great time for me to really get close to Pam's dad. He is in heaven now, but he was a wonderful person who had tremendous wisdom. He became a member of our finance committee, and to this day I miss his input.

As Pam and I made various preparations to leave Tulsa, I had made a budget and list of priorities. I know what I'm about to say would seem like it would be impossible for most people to do, but for me it wasn't impossible.

I had budgeted everything with one exception. I don't know how I did it, but I forgot to include in our budget a U-Haul truck. When I first realized it, I didn't want to tell Pam. Even I couldn't understand how I forgot to do that.

I thought to myself, "Oh well, it can't be that much."

I was wrong. It was almost eight hundred dollars. Now I'm thinking I'm in trouble. We didn't have an extra eight hundred dollars. I remember crying out to the Lord and sharing with Him that He knew my heart and I didn't intentionally not budget the truck, but I didn't know what to do.

Within a few days I had a check delivered to me for one thousand dollars to help us. It was an answer to prayer that not only covered the cost of the truck, but also gave us a little left over. Thank You, Jesus! Truly, God will supply all of our needs!

You may be hearing something in your spirit right now, and you aren't sure how you could afford to do it. That was one of my greatest concerns. How can I afford to budget expenditures that are coming when I don't have the finances to do it?

I have learned over the years that this is where faith comes in. Not only faith to do what He is calling you to do no matter how much it is out of your comfort zone, but also to realize that you are trusting God to supply all of your needs in the process.

I knew I was obeying God with this new venture, and I relied heavily on the following word from the Old Testament again:

"Now it shall come to pass, if you diligently obey the voice of the Lord your God, to observe carefully all His commandments which I command you today, that the Lord your God will set you high above all the nations of the earth. And all these blessings shall come upon you and overtake you, because you obey the voice of the Lord your God."

(DEUTERONOMY 28:1-2)

When Pam and I did finally load the truck and drive back to Lafayette, we had an interesting welcome at one of the first places we stopped. Even though we were going to be living with Pam's mom and dad, I was keeping my eye open for something we could afford to rent once we had the finances.

I had stopped at a real estate office in Lafayette to inquire if there were any homes for rent, sharing that we were not in a position to buy at this time. As I shared with the receptionist our desire, I also gave her my name and told her my wife and I were starting a new church in Lafayette.

I will never forget her reply, "Are you the same Bill Mickler who graduated from Jefferson High School?"

"Yes."

"And you are a pastor?"

"Yes."

Her quick response to my yes was, "My God, there's hope for all of us!"

Her response really surprised me. "Do I know you?"

"Yes, we graduated together."

Well, we had a nice conversation, and it was obvious from that conversation that she was still amazed that I was going to be a pastor of a church. What she did not say but was thinking was obvious.

She was thinking, how in the world can a guy like I knew in high school, doing the things I, and others, knew he did, be a minister.

She wasn't thinking anything different about me than I had thought about myself. Truly an amazing journey and greeting back into my hometown.

A local realtor and friend helped us find the first sight for our new church, to be called Victory Christian Center. It was actually the basement of a local bank. The president of the bank approved the lease through the realtor, but I felt I needed to meet the president and explain the vision of our church. I really felt strongly in my spirit I was to meet with him before we signed the lease.

The meeting went very well. He was extremely supportive, gave us a very low monthly rent, and at the conclusion of our meeting gave the church a five hundred dollar check to remodel the basement. He didn't know this, but we didn't have any funds to remodel the basement for the start of our church.

Over the years I have learned to trust God's word, and to trust that He directs my steps.

"The steps of a righteous man are ordered of the Lord and He delights in his way."

(PSALM 37:28)

As I have described earlier, I did not really want to return to Lafayette, because there were still many giants in the land. It became much more difficult than I had imagined, and I soon realized that the healing work I thought God had done in my life was still an ongoing project.

My saving grace was number one knowing that in spite of how I felt, I was in the center of the will of God, and number two, seeing people receive Jesus and get set free. That part of the ministry was wonderful.

Deep within my heart I felt when we began our church, that all of our children living in Lafayette would be a part of our ministry. Well, that was a great thought, but it never happened. My children never did become a part of the church. It was, and remains, a big disappointment.

I share this with you because there are times in all of our lives when we release our faith for certain things to happen, only realizing that it appears never to happen. My encouragement is to never give up regarding what you are believing for, but also, be encouraged to continue to move forward with what God is showing you.

It has been my experience that many people allow past hurts and disappointment to define their future. This is a trap from the devil. If you do not deal with disappointments quickly, they soon become discouragements, and then they become full blown depression. Do not allow yourself to remain disappointed!

As I shared in an earlier chapter of this book, regardless of what you see, get your hopes up. Hope will never disappoint. Do not lose your hope!

The chapter of this section of the book is "Deny Yourself and Follow Jesus." Over my almost forty years of ministry, I would say that is excellent advice. Another way to put it might be, get over yourself, focus on Jesus and move forward with what He has shown you to accomplish.

One thing I know for sure. If I can get over how I'm feeling about myself and focus on Jesus, I can accomplish His will, but when I'm thinking about the hurt and disappointment in my life, I'm not moving forward with Jesus.

Our focus should always be on Jesus!

"Since we are surrounded by so great a cloud of witnesses let us lay aside every weight, and the sin which so easily ensnares us, and let us run with endurance the race that is set before us, looking unto Jesus, the author and finisher of our faith, who for the joy that was set before Him endured the

cross, despising the shame, and has sat down at the right hand of the throne of God."

(HEBREWS 12:1-2)

We deny ourselves, pick up our cross, and follow Jesus. That is our assignment on this earth. Totally denying self-will, but with all our love and determination, seeking His will for our lives.

I know that this is a very strong statement, but I believe it is God's will. Nothing should come before the leading of the Holy Spirit in our lives. The leading of the Holy Spirit is the perfect will for each of us, and some day we will look back over our lives and give an account.

My question to you is, are you currently operating in the center of the will of God for your life? Are you following the Holy Spirit, or are you in control? If you are in control, then it is because you have not denied yourself. The good news is it is not too late to change.

The vision of our church is to share the love, acceptance and forgiveness of Jesus with everyone. It is that love and acceptance, and forgiveness that changed my life, and if it hasn't changed yours already, it will.

Jesus came to set people free, and if we aren't thinking about ourselves, then we can be about His business helping hurting people. I love what Jesus had to share about His mission in the book of Luke:

"The Spirit of the Lord is upon Me, because He has anointed Me to preach the gospel to the poor; He has sent Me to heal

the brokenhearted. To proclaim liberty to the captives and recovery of sight to the blind. To set at liberty those who are oppressed; To proclaim the acceptable year of the Lord."

(LUKE 4:18-19)

My experience is that almost everyone I have ever met has experienced one of the above challenges in their life. The answer to each challenge is Jesus. You and I have the answer for everyone experiencing any of these challenges in the world, and if we are not thinking about ourselves, then we can truly be about our Father's business as Jesus was.

Ask yourself a revealing question. When is the last time you led someone to Jesus? When was the last time you told someone about Jesus? When was the last time you shared your testimony with someone, realizing what you have already been through might just save their life?

Whether you realize it or not, we are all on assignment from God during our life on this earth. You are either living that assignment or you are not. The choice is not God's or your families or your friends. The choice is yours, and it is never too late to make the right choice.

If I focus on all the things in my life that didn't work out the way I had hoped they would, I can become very, very disappointed. I wish I could tell you I never do that, but it wouldn't be true. Sometimes I have a pity party.

I have heard it said that when you throw a pity party, you are the only one who shows up. That isn't true in my experience. When you throw a pity party, the devil always shows up to encourage you as to how bad things are. The best way to stop the party is to deny yourself and throw the devil out.

On the other hand, when I stop to think about all the people who have had their lives changed through the healing power of Jesus through the ministry God directed us to have, I am overwhelmed with joy. So many lives have been touched by Jesus through my wife and I following the leading of the Holy Spirit.

I certainly agree with the real estate receptionist when I arrived in her office looking for a place to rent, "My God there is hope for all of us!"

She was speaking her experience with me, but I also believe she was speaking the word of God…there truly is hope for all of us. Each of us should be carriers of that hope.

Remember, we are on assignment from God, so go forth realizing that you have within you the power of God's Son through the leading of the Holy Spirit to make a difference in the life of every person you meet.

By denying ourselves and following Jesus we can truly:

"MAKE THE BEST OF THE REST"

11

WHERE IS THE SUDAN?

Victory in Lafayette prospered, and the church continued to grow. It has been an awesome time of watching and being a part of literally hundreds and hundreds of people having their lives impacted by the power of the word of God and His healing restoration. It has been awesome.

Our church has always been involved in missions. I know that was the leading of the Holy Spirt, but we were also influenced heavily by Pastors Billy Joe and Sharon Daugherty. Victory in Tulsa was an outreach church, especially in missions.

When we started the church we had a few supported missionaries that we knew through the ministry in Tulsa. Most were supported by a few hundred dollars monthly.

During that period of time I would have every request from missionaries and other organizations placed on my desk for prayer. I would pray over the request and ask the Lord if I was to do anything. Most of the time I didn't really hear anything, but sometimes I would hear a dollar amount to send. Sometimes it would be a somewhat small amount in comparison to what they needed, but I knew that if they had a huge mailing list multiplied by the amount I sent, it could possibly meet the need.

One day I was doing what I just described when I came across a letter from a missionary friend I knew in Tulsa. The letter described a need to build an orphanage in the Sudan, and, described the horror of years of war and how it had left so many orphans. The need shared in the letter was for twelve thousand dollars to build a dormitory for orphans in Yei, South Sudan.

The letter really seemed to catch my attention, but I just prayed over it like I did all the rest.

What I heard shocked me: "I want you to build the dormitory."

"Wow! God is that really you?"

"Yes, I want you to build the dormitory."

I continued to pray until I had a total peace that God was asking us to build the dormitory. What I didn't have a peace about was the fact that we didn't have twelve thousand dollars to build the dorm. As a matter of fact, we were in a fairly tight spot financially at the time.

I finally settled the issue that this was a project God wanted us to be involved with. I had a peace in my spirit that the assignment was from God, but I was wondering where the financial means would be coming from. I knew they would be coming from God, but how would He do it?

The story I'm about to tell you is to give all the glory to God, but also to share with you that He will use anyone who will do what He asks, and He will supply all the needs based on His abilities and our faith in Him.

I knew I would need to share this with my wife and the finance committee in addition to our staff and church, but I also knew that I would have to have a plan for the vision to build the dormitory. I knew that if God wanted us to finance the project, He would show us how to do it.

The answer for the prayer as to how to raise the money came very quickly. I felt the Lord said to have a golf tournament at one of the golf courses. We would contact local businesses and individuals to have them advertise on each of the holes. In addition, we would have some revenue from the participants in the actual golf tournament.

It was a total team effort for our church, and everyone was excited as we shared the vision to help build a dormitory for orphans in the Sudan. Everyone worked really hard to raise the twelve thousand dollars.

Remember in the previous chapter I shared how we are all on assignment from God. God will always supply all our needs when we are doing what He has called us to do.

Sometimes I reflect back on my experience in the Marine Corps in relationship to all of our needs being met. In the Marine Corps, and I'm sure this is true in any branch of our armed forces, you receive your orders. They are detailed and give you definitive instructions and dates.

Once you receive the orders you expect all of your needs to be met. You have faith you will have the proper clothing, weapons, equipment, housing, transportation, food, etc., etc., etc. You expect all of this because you have received your orders. You don't think about how you are going to pay for everything or make everything happen.

Wouldn't it be nice if we had the same faith attitude toward God? Okay God, I know you're going to supply all my needs. I won't be anxious or worried about anything, because I know you are in charge, and I'm carrying out your orders for me.

I think this is how it should be for all of us. No worry, no anxiety, no fear, no doubt, no unbelief, just faith in God to supply all of our needs because we are on an assignment from Him carrying out His orders.

The evening before the golf tournament we had raised eleven thousand dollars. Wow! I was excited. We needed twelve thousand, but in my mind eleven thousand was close enough. I knew we could figure something out to come up with just the other thousand needed.

That evening I had to make a trip to Walmart. As I was leaving a lady came in with her grandson and asked how I was doing and how was the church going. I shared with her we were having a golf tournament the following morning to build a dormitory in the Sudan for orphans. She shared her grandson was a golfer and could he play. I told her yes, gave them the times and left.

The following morning, we were all at the opening tee when the lady's grandson arrived. We assigned him a team and a cart, and after we prayed, I went to my cart. A few minutes later the ladies' grandson came running over to me and said he forgot to give me something from his grandmother.

I will never forget that moment. As I opened the envelop there was a thousand-dollar check. The first group had not yet teed off, and we had the twelve thousand dollars needed. Thank You, Jesus!

As a result of that twelve thousand dollars raised and our interest in the project, I was invited to travel with the missionary to Juba, South Sudan where a ministry crusade was scheduled in addition to food distribution through Feed The Hungry.

In praying about the invitation, I felt the Lord leading me to participate. I wasn't even sure where the Sudan was. I knew it was in Africa, but I had to get out a map to find out exactly where.

God may not send you to the Sudan, but I guarantee he has an exciting assignment for you if you'll accept. I had no idea how exciting this assignment would eventually become.

Myself, and another man from our church traveled with our missionary friend to Juba, South Sudan. The country had been at war for several years, basically between the north, which is primarily Muslim and the south which is primarily Christian.

It was quite obvious the area had been at war. There were burned out vehicles, some civilian, some military, giant craters in the roads, and in general what looked like a war-torn country. I have never seen anything quite like it.

The crusade outreach was awesome with thousands of people attending, thousands also giving their lives to the Lord, and many, many miracles. It was an awesome sight to behold, but one of the most important events that took place also was my introduction to a man from Yei, South Sudan who pastored a church there and had the vision from the Lord to start the orphanage in Yei.

I believe that God wanted me in Juba to meet Pastor Stanley Lo Nathan, the man I just described to you. When we met, I believe there was an instant connection in the realm of the spirit. There are divine connections that God has orchestrated for all of us, and if we will allow Him to position us, we will make those connections.

It was during this time in the Sudan that I was able to hear first-hand from the man to whom God had given the vision for the orphanage to be called the Dreamland Children's Home. At the time I thought the orphanage was a vision that the missionary I traveled with had, but I learned that Pastor Stanley was the man with the vision.

In further meetings with Stanley in Yei I learned more about his background. I learned that he had led a life away from the Lord as a younger man and traveled to Cairo for schooling and work. To my amazement he shared with me the story of how he gave his life to Jesus.

It happened one day that on a street corner in Cairo, he met a lady who had started a Bible school in Cairo. She invited Stanley and one of his friends. This is the amazing part, the Bible school was Victory Bible Institute, and the leader of the school was a graduate of the school from Tulsa, Oklahoma. The very Bible school that I once directed. Totally a divine appointment from God for Stanley.

It was part of the vision of Victory Bible Institute in Tulsa to train up faithful men and women of God who would go forth into the world and train others.

"And the things that you have heard from me among many witnesses, commit these to faithful men who will be able to teach others also."

(2 TIMOTHY 2:2)

It was so exciting for me to see the vision of Pastor Billy Joe and Sharon actually happening in Cairo, Egypt and Yei, South Sudan. I had prayed and really wondered why I felt led in my spirit to travel all the way to the Sudan when I wasn't really needed. After meeting and spending time with Stanley, I knew.

As Stanley shared the vision for the Dreamland Children's Home, I felt in my spirit that our church was to come alongside him and assist with the finances.

The exact words I heard were, "I want you to come alongside Stanley and help establish cash flow for him."

I must admit I questioned if that could really be a word from the Lord for me. My background as a businessman understood cash flow. If you have cash flow you can accomplish quite a bit, but without it there isn't much you can do. I didn't want my business background to get in the way of the leading of the Holy Spirit.

I finally settled the issue believing that it was God's will for us to assist Stanley. I have heard many stories where people in impoverished nations around the world had a church from another country come in and take over the vision that the local minister had, making them almost a servant or employee of that ministry. I never liked that and still don't.

Stanley and I had a long talk about the vision he had from the Lord, what he had endured to follow Jesus through the war, famine and poverty, and how God continued to show Himself strong on Stanley's behalf. It was a powerful testimony.

I began to make plans to come to Yei and see the land he felt the Lord had given him for the Dreamland Children's Home. It took almost a year for me to get there, but I was eventually able to visit Yei and walk the land that would eventually become the Dreamland Children's Home. When that happened, Stanley would show me as we walked the land where the various buildings would be. He even had drawn up blueprints.

Pastor Stanley had the vision from God, and he knew exactly what God wanted him to do. As our relationship in the Lord developed, I continued to hear that we, at Victory in Lafayette, were to come alongside him assisting with the finances that were needed. I really felt this was God's project, and I knew that if He wanted us involved, He would supply all the needs through whom He decided to use to help Stanley.

I found myself asking Stanley a question. As I asked the question, it really even surprised me, because I was not even consciously thinking it. The question seemed to come out of nowhere, but in retrospect, I really think it came from God.

The question was, "Stanley, what would you do if you had fifty thousand dollars?"

Stanley's response was, "Where would I get that?"

We both smiled and laughed at my question and his response to the question, however, he did share with me in detail how he would use the finances.

During my trip back to America, all I could think about was supplying the financial needs for the visionary to run with God's project. Everywhere I went when I was in Juba and Yei, Sudan, there were children. Stanley had told me that there were thousands of orphans in the Sudan due to all the killing that took place during the war years. I know God penetrated my heart with the need.

Stanley and I had discussed the tremendous need that was in the Yei, South Sudan area for an orphanage. It was decided that the first group would number twelve, and then we would grow quickly from there based on facilities and finances.

When I returned to Victory in Lafayette, Indiana, I shared the vision with our leadership and staff to be sure we were all in agreement. Everyone was in agreement to help build the orphanage and come along side Pastor Stanley, but I'm not sure everyone was in agreement when I told them that I felt we were to raise fifty thousand dollars for facilities that would include dormitories, classrooms, clothing, school supplies, and the list just went on and on. It was actually quite long.

I share all of this with you because God wants us all involved somewhere helping His people. He is just looking for those who will say, here I am Lord, use me however you would like. Then He will take you out of your comfort zone and give you the tremendous blessing of watching His supernatural provision flow.

The commitment was made to come alongside Stanley in birthing the Dreamland Children's Home, but now I needed the leading of the Holy Spirit as to how He would have us raise the finances.

I knew if I was following the leading of the Holy Spirit, not only would He lead me and our church to be involved, but He would show us how to raise the finances.

I remember asking the Lord how He wanted us to do it. I heard the following: "Putt-Putt Golf." Immediately I saw in my mind the Putt-Putt Golf Course we had near our local mall. It had three eighteen-hole courses, and, would be perfect for the outreach to raise the fifty thousand dollars.

In just a matter of minutes the Holy Spirit showed me how to organize the entire project, including the people to be involved in the various leadership roles. It was truly exciting. I was pumped and ready to go!

Now it was time to talk to the various people who would be involved, including the owner of the Putt-Putt course. As I proceeded to go through my list of priorities with the various people, I found they were all not quite as excited as I was. That doesn't mean they weren't in agreement, they just hadn't been to the Sudan and observed the tremendous need. In addition, they hadn't heard the vision that I heard from Stanley.

The reason I have shared this part with you about people sometimes not being quite as excited as you are about what God has shown you, is that they haven't necessarily heard it first-hand from God like you have. You can't expect everyone you talk with and share a vision with to be as excited and passionate as you are, but the more you share with them, the more they will desire to be involved. Your compassion can be very contagious, but you must be sure to not let the lack of passion in others affect you.

My first encounter with what I just described to you happened with the owner of the Putt-Putt Course. I asked him if it would be possible for me to lease his facility for an all-day event on a Saturday. I told him we were going to raise funds to build an orphanage in the Sudan.

He thought about it for a moment, and then said he would for what I thought was a very reasonable few hundred dollars. I told him that amount would be fine, and we set a date. He then asked me how much I was planning to raise. When I told him, the entire expression on his face changed.

"You'll never be able to raise that amount."

Well, that was encouraging, and then he proceeded to explain to me in detail why I couldn't do what I felt God told me to do. He had a compelling list of reasons why it wouldn't work to raise the amount that was our goal, and they all appeared to be very logical.

He was really a nice man, and I don't think he was trying to discourage me as much as he was trying to prepare me so that I wouldn't be disappointed that the fifty thousand dollars was out of the realm of possibility.

In my years of ministry, I am continually amazed at how many people feel it is there job to be sure and tell others they can't do what they feel God is showing them to do. It isn't that these people are bad, they are just on a mission to keep people they care about from being disappointed.

My response has always been, what's the big deal about being disappointed? Learn to deal with it and move on. Everyone needs to learn to deal with disappointment, not live their lives trying to avoid disappointment. If you try something and it doesn't work, learn from it and move one. Too many people never try anything, avoiding the disappointments in life, but also missing the tremendous victories God has for us.

I came away from the meeting with the owner of the course thinking that what he shared made sense, but also thinking that I am on an assignment from God, and if this is really His assignment, then every need will be provided. Failure is never an option if we are following God's leading.

When the Dreamland Children's Home Putt-Putt Golf Tournament had ended, God had provided just over fifty thousand dollars. It was an amazing event, all of our people who participated were blessed, we now had the finances to really escalate the building of the orphanage, and in all of this, all the glory goes to God!

Needless to say, Pastor Stanley was excited. God had supplied for the vision He had given Stanley several years earlier.

Always remember that God's will is to take us from glory to glory while supplying all of our needs, but also continually taking us beyond our comfort zone. I can honestly tell you, that even though I was excited, passionate, and very emotional about helping Stanley birth the orphanage for these precious children, I was also from time to time fighting a fight of faith against fear.

Yes, I know this sounds like a contradiction to faith, but sometimes I think we can feel like a failure if we admit we feel fear. I don't believe this is true. Personally I think we all feel fear from time to time. It isn't in the feeling of fear that is our challenge; I believe our challenge is in our decision making process of thought to focus on the mission and rebuke the contradiction that comes from entertaining a fear of failure. Anyone who consistently entertains a fear of failure will eventually fail.

One of my favorite scriptures comes from 2 Timothy:

"For God has not given us a spirit of fear, but of power, love and a sound mind."

(2 TIMOTHY 2:7)

I again will admit to you that on many occasions I feel fear try to invade my mind. I felt a little fearful apprehension when God was speaking to me to help build the first dormitory in the Sudan. I felt it again when I was invited to go to a war-torn country where some fighting was still taking place. I felt it as I described earlier when I felt we were to commit to raising the fifty thousand dollars.

What if it isn't God? What if I fail? What if no one wants to help me? Who am I to do this? I don't have any experience? What if…. What if…. What if….

Whenever I feel fear I almost always think of the above scripture. I don't have fear, that is an attribute of the devil. I have power, love, and a sound mind. Therefore, I refuse fear, and I will continue to the best of my ability to follow the leading of the Holy Spirit. You do the same!

Sometimes people say, "Well I tried to do something for God, and it didn't work. Maybe it wasn't God after all." I think that has happened to all of us. In the case that this has perhaps happened to you, just learn from it and move on. Don't stop following what you think is the leading of the Holy Spirit.

I know I have used this scripture earlier in the book, but it is also appropriate to use here. I love this word:

"And we know that all things work together for good to those who love God, to those who are called according to His purpose."

(ROMANS 8:28)

I have shared many times over the years with our church, and while it is humorous, I also think it is very true: "If all of us learned something every time we made a mistake, most of us should be brilliant by now."

So, after we had raised twelve thousand dollars for the first dormitory, we now had fifty thousand dollars ready to help expedite the growth of the infrastructure of the Dreamland in addition to supplies and staff. I made several trips over to visit and plan with Stanley. It was an awesome time.

It didn't take long to begin to work our way through the fifty thousand dollars, and one day I was praying just asking the Lord to show me whatever He had for me. I wasn't praying about the Sudan or anything else, just asking God to show me what He wanted me to know.

In my spirit I heard, "Ask Stanley what he would do with one hundred thousand dollars."

I can't say I was overly excited about hearing that. I'm not even sure I wanted to hear that. I still remember some people complaining about the last fund raiser that they felt they did most of the work. All I thought when I would hear a few complaints was, how can you be concerned about how much work you are doing when it is to touch the lives of precious children and bring glory to God. Who cares how hard you have to work? (Sorry, some of my Marine Corps sympathy is showing.)

The more I prayed asking God to please confirm to me that this is an assignment from Him, the more I felt secure that it was. I have found that when our heart is pure before God, that He will do everything in His power to confirm to us what He is showing us.

Now I was ready to do it all over again with our leaders, staff and congregation.

Back to the owner of the Putt-Putt Course. He was in agreement again for us to lease the course for a day. He was amazed at the goal of one hundred thousand dollars, but he wasn't adamant in his questioning the amount. He remembered what happened the last time.

The format for this outreach was very similar to our last, but I personally made a mistake. I didn't think it was a mistake when I made it, but later I realized I made a decision without consulting the Holy Spirit.

Have you ever done that? My guess is you have. We are all creatures of habit, good or bad. It is important that we become so disciplined that we do not make decisions based on a quick response, but, based on the leading of the Holy Spirit.

I made a quick response and I believe it caused us to miss our goal. It was my fault. Instead of hitting the goal of one hundred thousand, we were able to raise seventy thousand. To God be the glory for the seventy thousand, and I learned a very valuable lesson that I will never forget.

I know I shared this earlier, but if every mistake we make becomes a valuable lesson, a teachable moment for us by the Holy Spirit, then we don't beat ourselves up with feeling bad, we just repent, learn and move on realizing that the next time we will do a better job of consulting and following the leading of the Holy Spirit.

As I reflect back on the letter that crossed my desk many years earlier describing the desire of a man to build an orphanage in the Sudan, I wonder what might have happened if I had been in a hurry and had not been seeking the leading of the Holy Spirit. Would God have found someone else for the project?

Possibly. Could the project have never been completed? Possibly. Could Stanley never have been able to implement the vision God had given him? Possibly. Could the children who are now growing to maturity in their relationship with God have died a premature death in the villages and bush areas of the Sudan? Possibly.

On the other hand, perhaps God would have found someone else to do what He had originally planned for us to do.

I'll probably never know the answer to this, but I am so thankful to God that He gave us the assignment at Victory.

I hope my reflecting on what God has done through Victory Christian Center in Lafayette, Indiana for support of the vision God had given to Pastor Stanley for the Dreamland Children's Home doesn't come across as trying to show what we have done. I am reflecting on it here, to show you what God has done.

Thank You, Jesus, for the opportunity to be involved with the Dreamland Children's Home in Yei, South Sudan that has grown to 130 orphans.

What God Has Provided: (Accumulated Giving Through October 2018)

........$226,540	Buildings and Infrastructure
..........572,630	Accumulative Orphan Monthly Support
..........180,752	Dreamland Staff Salaries
............66,800	Vehicles
............26,213	Christmas Gifts
............23,650	Special Projects
............15,406	Miscellaneous
..............4,000	Purdue University and South Sudan Government Memorandum of Understanding with Purdue to Engage Agriculturally in South Sudan
..............2,150	Operation Joseph Farm Project
$1,118,141	To the Glory of God!!

I close this chapter by sharing with you that there are many Stanley's in the world who have a vision from God, and God will bring people alongside them who can help, through God, to support the vision they have been given.

Be sure to be open to the leading of the Holy Spirit, because it is never too late to get involved in God's work to touch people with the love of Jesus. Above all, I know that God wants you to be involved and to:

"*MAKE THE BEST OF THE REST*"

12

STAY FOCUSED!

It has been my experience over my years in ministry that if you can keep focused on the word of God and the leading of the Holy Spirit in addition to being obedient and discipled to both by walking by faith and not by sight, that you will have a great life.

I think the following scriptures sum this up:

"Therefore, we also since we are surrounded by so great a cloud of witnesses let us lay aside every weight, and the sin which so easily ensnares us, and let us run with endurance the race that is set before us, looking unto Jesus, the author and finisher of our faith, who for the joy that was set before Him endured the cross, despising the shame, and has sat down at the right hand of the throne of God."

(HEBREWS 12:1-2)

"If you are willing and obedient, you shall eat the good of the land."

(ISAIAH 1:19)

It is impossible to over emphasize the importance of living the word of God. The written word of God is always there for us, and the current word God wants to show us is delivered by the Holy Spirit. Our victory is walked out by faith, by living God's word.

One of the greatest examples of this is when Jesus was led by the Holy Spirit into the wilderness. It was a further step in the earthly walk of Jesus immediately after He was baptized by John the Baptist in the Jordan River. By fasting for forty days and nights, Jesus would be in a weakened physical condition, but spiritually He was busy living the word of God, in addition to being the Word of God.

His response when He was confronted in the wilderness is the same as our response should be. Jesus knew the power of the word of God, and so should we.

The devil came to tempt Jesus, just as he continually does to each of us.

The devil said to Jesus, "If you are the Son of God, command these stones to become bread."

The devil always wants to plant thoughts in our mind to get us to take action on his words instead of the word of God. This is exactly what happened in the Garden of Eden with Adam and Eve. This technique is what caused sin to enter into God's perfect creation, and it continues to be the method the enemy uses.

The devil knew Jesus had fasted forty days and forty nights. Jesus was hungry as the word states in Matthew 4:2, but the response of Jesus to the devil was not one based on natural hunger, it was one based on the power of the word of God.

"Away with you, Satan! For it is written, 'You shall worship the Lord your God, and Him only you shall serve.'"

(MATTHEW 4:10)

In my life since receiving Jesus as my Lord and Savior, I have had many times when I would make decisions based on a quick impulse or thought, but without the clarity of the word of God. It is impossible to have the faith described in the Bible without the clarity of God's word.

Once you know for sure what the word of God is speaking into your spirit, you are ready to boldly move forward, fully knowing God has gone ahead to prepare the way with all you will need.

Abraham is a great example of staying focused on God's word. It doesn't mean he didn't make a few errors along the way, just like all of us, but he remained true to what God had shown him in a vision.

"Get out of your country, from your family, and from your Father's house, to a land I will show you. I will make you a great nation, and I will bless you and make your name great and you shall be a blessing. I will bless those who bless you, and I will curse those who curse you, and in you all the families of the earth shall be blessed."

(GENESIS 12:1-3)

The life of Abraham is really summed up in the book of Romans. He began his journey when he was seventy-five years of age, and he never looked back. He trusted God, that whatever God said is the way it would be. This is the type of faith all of us should pursue.

> *"Abraham did not waver at the promise of God through unbelief, but was strengthened in faith, giving glory to God and being fully convinced that what God had promised He was well able to perform."*
>
> (ROMANS 4:20-21)

All of us would like to have that type of faith that Abraham had. Fully convinced that God could do whatever He said He was going to do. Most of us really believe it, but sometimes we do not stay focused on what God said.

It takes continual discipline to focus on what we believe God said. If there is a number one thing missing in many people in the body of Christ, and my life as well, I believe it is a lack of discipline to do what we need to do.

When our total focus is on what we believe God said, there is no room for doubt and unbelief. When we entertain both of those we are stepping closer to the fear factor that exists in many people. Total focus on what God said will always allow us to stay focused.

My prayer journal and my Bible are the two most important items I am continually disciplined to carry with me wherever I go. Sometimes I forget them, and I feel it in my spirit. It's hard to describe, but without both I feel I am not really prepared for the day.

There are so many times in all our lives when we ask ourselves if we are really doing what God showed us to do. For me, I am constantly consulting with my prayer journal to reinforce my faith that I am doing what the Lord has shown me to do. Am I on the right path, or have I drifted off?

The Holy Spirit is always there for us to show us the direction for our life. Perhaps you are trying to determine the direction for your life at this very moment, or maybe you're faced with a decision you need to make, but you aren't sure what to do.

I have great news for you. God, through His precious Holy Spirit, wants to lead and guide you into His truth about whatever it is you are facing. In addition, He wants to continue to show you the direction He has for your life.

Never give up, and never consider giving in, other than to give in to the leading of God's Holy Spirit to lead and guide you into His truth continually. When this act of discipline and submission becomes your priority, you will begin to live a life of abundance and fulfillment with your total focus on God's will.

"When He, the Spirit of truth has come, He will guide you into all truth, for He will not speak on His own authority, but whatever He hears He will speak, and He will tell you things to come. He will glorify Me, for He will take what is Mine and declare it to you. All things the Father has are mine. Therefore, I said that He will take of mine and declare it to you."

(JOHN 16:13-15)

A great example of staying focused on the leading of the Holy Spirit happened in my life on a trip a few years ago to Lima, Peru. I had been asked by a good friend to travel to Lima with him and minister at several different locations in the area. One of our sons accompanied me us on the trip and also ministered.

On the flight to Lima I felt I had a word from the Lord involving something that would happen while I was on this trip. I felt the Lord said that something so miraculous would happen, and that I would know without a doubt it was from the Lord.

I made a note of it in my prayer journal, and, wondered what it might be. During the course of the meetings we saw many people give their hearts to the Lord, people were healed, and we saw the power of God touching lives as Jesus was lifted up. It was an awesome time of ministry, and during all the busy ministry part of the trip I had not given any thought about what the Lord had shown me about something happening so miraculous I would know only He could have orchestrated it. I realized all the miracles happening during the services were from the hand of God.

Toward the end of our trip the minister who had invited us to come to Lima shared that he wanted to walk around the town and try to find a gift store he had remembered from one of his previous trips. He wanted to buy a gift for his wife.

He asked if we wanted to go with him, and my son said yes, but I didn't want to go. I was looking forward to hanging out alone at the hotel and doing absolutely nothing. We had been with many people during the trip, and I was excited about the prospect of being alone.

As they prepared to leave, I began to feel a stirring in my spirit that I was to go with them. I have been sharing in this chapter about the importance of staying focused on the word of God and the leading of the Holy Spirit.

I must admit to you that I was trying to ignore what I thought might be the leading of the Holy Spirit trying to stir me that I was to go with them.

They were just about to leave the hotel when I felt very strongly in my spirit that I was to go with them. I finally asked them to wait a few minutes, that I would be going with them.

Our journey began with me not being really very happy, and I think that is probably an understatement. I wanted my time alone. I was probably pouting a little bit with God, thinking, but not really asking, why are you making me go shopping. I really don't want to go.

I finally settled the issue that this is obviously where God wanted me for the moment because the feeling to go with them would not leave me. As we began to walk around the town, I actually began to enjoy seeing the various sights. Lima is an exciting city estimated to have a population between eight and ten million people. There were times when it seemed like all of the population was on our street.

Our leader was having a difficult time finding the gift store as we traveled down one narrow street after the other, each crowded with gift stores and carts.

We had been searching for a long time, and our leader looking for the gift store he remembered suddenly realized he was totally lost.

No problem he stated. I'll just find a local Peruvian and they can direct us either to the gift store or back to the hotel, so we continued down a never-ending street seemingly getting more and more lost. Maybe I should have stayed back at the hotel, although getting lost has always been exciting for me.

We were walking by a small local eating establishment when a lady who looked Peruvian came out the door. I continued walking down the street, not really seeing the lady and the lady not really seeing me. Our leader and my son stopped and engaged her in conversation, and I continued walking to the end of the block looking around at the landscape, shops, and the multitude of people everywhere.

I finally stopped and looked around to see how they were doing, and could tell they were still deep in conversation. I decided to walk back and join them.

As I approached them, probably fifteen or twenty feet away, the lady looked up at me and started screaming: "It's you, it's you, it's you!" Then she started running toward me.

I had no idea what was happening, and neither did the others. I think they were as shocked and startled as I was.

She ran up to me, tears streaming down her face, continuing to scream: "It's you, it's you! God sent you!"

She threw her arms around me, continuing to sob and thank God. Then she grabbed my arm.

I am almost at a loss for words, when I somehow managed to say: "Do I know you?"

"Yes, yes! Your church in America. I've been to your church!"

"You've been to my church?"

"Yes, yes! Your wife, she leads worship, she sings, she dances. It is in Indiana. Yes, yes, I've been to your church!"

"You are an answer to prayer. God has sent you. Please come with me, I must talk with you alone."

I think now I was at a total loss for words. She told the others to stay where they were, and walked me to the end of the street, tightly embracing my arm as if she thought I might try to get away.

I again asked her is she really had been to our church, and she explained she had. She had been to a conference at Notre Dame in South Bend, Indiana, had made a trip to Lafayette, Indiana and someone had told her about our church.

She then explained how she had a terrible family situation, and, had asked God to please send her someone who would help her and pray for her. As I looked into her face with tears streaming down, I heard the same words in my spirit that I heard on the plane flying to Lima:

"You'll see something so miraculous that you will know that only I could have orchestrated it."

The lady then began to tell me the horrible story about what her family was going through, and would I please pray for her and her family. She said she that she knew God had answered her prayers by sending me.

I prayed for her and her family, encouraged her, and embraced eventually going our separate ways. For all of us, it was an astounding, miraculous experience, and we all knew only God could have orchestrated it. The moment taught me a valuable lesson, and that was to always stay focused on the leading of the Holy Spirit in all of our decisions.

There was nothing wrong with me staying at the hotel and resting, but I hadn't really prayed about it. I hadn't consulted the leading of the Holy Spirit. I hadn't really asked God. What if I hadn't been open to the Holy Spirit speaking into my spirit? What if I had ignored that still small inner voice?

I am continually encouraging our church and myself to constantly live the word of God and be led by the Holy Spirit. This is the truth, and once you know the truth and live the truth, you will have one action-packed, exciting life.

The Holy Spirit gave me this confession several years ago, and I continue to have our congregation confess it every time I minister. It would be good for you also:

"The word of God is truth. If I live the word I will be blessed. If I don't, I won't, it's just that simple."

It is so important that we stay focused on the word of God and the leading of His Spirit in everything we do. Let this become a habit with you, and your life will take on new meaning in everything you do because God has some super-natural encounters for you also.

"MAKE THE BEST OF THE REST"

13

AVOID DISTRACTIONS

Everything that God does is perfect. We have been created to project the image of God in all that we do. There is no imperfection in God, but because of what happened in the Garden of Eden man has been subjected to much distraction. It is important to realize, however, that God's original intent for mankind has not changed.

> *"Let us make man in Our image, according to Our likeness and let them have dominion over the fish of the sea, over the birds of the air, and over the cattle, over all the earth and over every creeping thing that creeps on the earth."*
>
> (GENESIS 1:26)

> *"So, God created man in His own image, in the image of God He created him male and female He created them."*
>
> (GENESIS 1:27)

"Then God blessed them and God said to them: 'Be fruitful and multiply, fill the earth and subdue it, have dominion over the fish of the sea, over the birds of the air, and over every living thing that moves on the earth.'"

(GENESIS 1:28)

It was God's original intent for mankind to resemble Him in every way. Man was created as a spiritual being, spirit, soul and body in the image of Almighty God to live in the Garden of Eden and fellowship with God. In doing so, mankind through God's original creation, Adam and Eve, would have total dominion and authority, just as God said.

It is hard to believe that Adam and Eve actually walked and talked with God. They lived in a perfect habitation created for them by God so that they could fellowship with Him and He could fellowship with His creation.

It was a perfect world that God had created. Man would have total dominion over everything that was on the face of the earth. Power, authority and dominion was delegated to God's creation. A perfect world created by a perfect God. This was God's original plan.

Apparently, the fallen angel, Lucifer, was on the earth during this period of time. We don't know everything about him, but we do know that he was thrown out of heaven by God along with many angels for rebelling against God. Regardless of exactly where he was and what he was doing is not relevant at this time, because we know, from the word of God, that man had complete dominion over everything on the earth, and that would include Lucifer, the devil.

God is always looking out for His creation. He wants to give us instructions to keep us safe and to position us where we can be blessed by Him. God is a loving, caring father, and He loves to bless His creation if we will just listen to Him and follow His instructions.

It is somewhat hard for us to imagine this, but Adam and Eve had but one instruction of what not to do, directly from God as far as we know from scripture in Genesis. That instruction was to not eat from one specific tree in the Garden.

"Of every tree of the garden you may freely eat, but of the tree of the knowledge of good and evil, you shall not eat, for in that day that you eat of it, you shall surely die."

(GENESIS 1:17)

What did Eve do when the devil came disguised as a serpent and tempted Eve to eat of the tree that was forbidden to her? She decided to focus on what the devil said. She became distracted from God's original intent, and then in her distraction, she convinced her husband to be distracted also.

"The serpent said to Eve, 'Has God indeed said, You shall not eat of every tree in the garden?' And the woman said to the serpent, 'We may eat the fruit of the trees in the garden, but the fruit which is in the midst of the garden, God has said, You shall not eat of it, nor shall you touch it, lest you die.'"

(GENESIS 3:1-3)

The devil then contradicted the word of God by telling Eve she would not die if she took of the fruit of the tree. Eve listened to the serpent and turned away from God's direction. She then convinced Adam to do the same and turn away also.

This caused a separation between God and man and was the first example of sin that entered into mankind. Into the flesh of man entered sin through the forbidden fruit. It was at this moment that the spirit of man died.

Man was still soul and flesh, but the spirit of man would be dead until our Lord and Savior would come to give us a new life in the realm of the spirit. God is Spirit, and we were created in the image of God. When our spirit man died, the sin nature of the world took over.

This is why it is so important that we accept Jesus as our Lord and Savior. This is how our sins are taken away and our spirit becomes reborn. It is described in the book of John in a conversation between the Pharisee Nicodemus, a ruler of the Jews, and Jesus. Nicodemus acknowledged that God was obviously with Jesus because of the signs that Jesus did.

> *"Jesus answered and said to Nicodemus, 'Most assuredly, I say to you, unless one is born again, he cannot see the kingdom of God.' Nicodemus said to Jesus, 'How can a man be born when he is old? Can a man enter a second time into his mother's womb and be born?' Jesus answered, 'Most assuredly, I say to you, unless one is born of water and the Spirit, he cannot enter the kingdom of God. That which is born of the flesh is flesh, and that which is born of the Spirit is spirit.'"*

> (JOHN 3:2-6)

Jesus was teaching a powerful message. God is Spirit, and man was created by God in His Spiritual image. Since man died a spiritual death in the garden, man had to be resurrected through the same power that resurrected Jesus from the dead, the very power of God Himself manifest through the power of the Holy Spirit.

When our time on this earth ends, it is our spirit and our soul that goes immediately to heaven to be with Jesus. Our flesh, which is the sin nature of man, does not make the trip. In heaven we will have a resurrected body. Thank You, Jesus. Sometimes I wonder what I will look like in heaven. I told my wife one day that maybe I'll look like my graduation picture from high school. I always liked that picture. She just laughed.

I shared all of this with you regarding the Garden of Eden because since the beginning of time, the beginning of God's creation, there have been distractions. Avoiding distractions is not as difficult as some people think, but it is very important that we admit that we can all be distracted.

I began this book by sharing from my own experience as to how we can all pursue something that in our right mind we would have never pursued. What happens is we become distracted by something that for a moment attracted us, but later we realized it was a total distraction. Some distractions can be somewhat minor, but I do believe some distractions have the potential to be deadly.

What are some of the distractions in your life? Things that seem to be pulling you away from the very thing God is trying to show you by the leading of His Spirit that you should be moving toward or away from. I am totally convinced that we are our own worst enemies when it comes to letting ourselves become distracted by the devil.

The same power, dominion and authority that Adam and Eve had is ours today through the victory Jesus gave us. If we are living the word of God, the devil will never be able to distract us. He will come and try to steal the word, but if we will continue to use that power, authority and dominion that God has given us through His Son and the power of His Holy Spirit, the devil will always flee.

"Submit to God, resist the devil and he will flee."

(JAMES 4:7)

There is a great example in the Bible regarding how deadly distraction can become. Keep in mind that we can all become distracted for a brief moment, but the longer you remain in a distracted state, the closer you move toward violating the will of God in your life and opening the door to the devil to steal, kill and destroy. Never, ever entertain distractions!

King David was a mighty man of God who is described by God as having a heart for God. It is obvious that he was at one time a humble shepherd boy who loved God. God hand picked David to eventually be king, and when that happened the people rejoiced.

King David was a great leader and his men loved him. He proved himself a mighty warrior in battle and it was obvious the hand of God was upon him. He gave the glory to God time and time again for his victories, and he truly appeared to be a man after God's own heart.

None of us are more that a moment away from a distraction presenting itself.

The Holy Spirit will always attempt to warn us, but if we aren't listening, the consequences as I stated earlier can be deadly.

Here is the story of King David, Bathsheba and Uriah. It truly does not fit the character of King David, but all of us can be vulnerable to the attack of the enemy if we will entertain his distraction.

I'll set the stage for the story. It takes place during a period of time when it is described as a time when Kings go to war. Apparently, there was a time of year that was best suited for war, probably has to do with weather conditions, but, on this particular occasion King David decided not to go with his men to battle.

We don't know the reason this happened because King David fought in many battles with his men. The only thing we know for sure is that on this occasion he decided to not go to war.

What we do know is that one evening King David arose from his bed and walked on the roof of his house. The rest is recorded history.

"And from the roof David saw a woman bathing, and the woman was beautiful to behold."

(2 SAMUEL 11:2)

We don't know exactly why King David didn't go to war. We really don't know why perhaps he couldn't sleep that night. For whatever reason as I paraphrase the rest of the story regarding King David, we know that when he saw Bathsheba bathing it was a major distraction, however, it was nothing that he did not have the power, authority and dominion over to get rid of.

Instead of going back to bed or doing something else to remove the distraction from his mind and flesh, he asked one of his attendants to find out who she was.

He was soon told that it was Bathsheba the wife of Uriah, one of David's trusted military men.

Next David sent for her, laid with her, and she became pregnant. David then sends for Uriah who was in battle. He tried to trick him into spending the night with his wife so that Uriah would think the child Bathsheba is pregnant with is Uriah's.

Uriah, being a loyal soldier and servant to David, said I cannot go to my wife when a battle is raging. I must return to my men. Obviously, Uriah was a very dedicated soldier to David. He returned to battle not knowing anything about what had transpired between David and his wife.

What happened next shows you just how deadly a distraction can become.

David sends for one of his military leaders. He shares a plot with the leader that will assure the death of Uriah, one of David's trusted military men. Because the word of the king was absolute during this time period, the order was carried out and Uriah was killed in battle.

It wasn't until David was confronted by the prophet Nathan that he finally came to his senses and repented before God. While the Lord did forgive David when he confessed, the sin which David's distraction allowed to happen opened the door for the devil and the enemies of God to blaspheme God.

So, David said to Nathan, "I have sinned against the Lord."
And Nathan said to David, "The Lord also has put away
your sin, you shall not die, however, because by this deed you
have given great occasion to the enemies of the Lord to blas-
pheme, the child also who is born to you shall surely die."

(2 SAMUEL 12:13-14)

What happened for David to have let this situation get so far out of hand that it ended with murder and death? Wasn't it David who was described by God as being a man after God's own heart? How could this happen to such a man?

I think something I heard from a town commissioner in Yei, South Sudan a few years ago is very appropriate here. It was a statement from a man who had known much hardship, with war, death and destruction. The meeting was between representatives of Purdue University and our Dreamland Children's Home visionary discussing the tremendous needs of the South Sudan.

This is when the commissioner spoke about the many challenges and situations that had developed creating much chaos and confusion. The statement that he made that so impressed me was as follows:

"We don't have time to learn from our own mistakes.
We must learn from the mistakes of others."

Why did David allow this to happen? Why did he turn an initial distraction into sin against God? How could a man of David's character allow this to happen? We too must learn from David's mistakes and the mistakes of others.

One thing I know for sure in my years of ministry, when you are totally focused on God, the opportunity to become distracted is diminished, but when you are focused on yourself, you are more vulnerable to the distractions this world offers.

"For where envy and self-seeking exist, confusion, and every evil thing are there."

(JAMES 3:16)

"For all that is in the world, the lust of the flesh, the lust of the eyes, and the pride of life, is not of the Father, but it is of the world."

(1 JOHN 2:16)

I was just reading a popular Christian magazine detailing the story of a pastor of a major mega church in America who had resigned his church do to a sexual encounter he had. In addition, I have known a few ministers personally who have had similar situations in their ministries. It happens way too frequently.

I believe things like these, and other things, happen to people when they lose sight of the main attraction in their lives. If Jesus is your main attraction, it is going to be very difficult for you to become distracted, but always remember that something is always being planned by your enemy to bring distraction into your life.

It may not be anything like I described above, but your enemy the devil has a variety of distractions he will try to use against you. If you are listening to the still small voice of the Holy Spirit, and if you are doing what the Holy Spirit is showing you to do, then you will probably never be distracted.

I'm amazed at the number of people I have counselled and ministered to over the years who with a little coaching have told me what they did wrong, how they knew it was wrong and how they did it anyway. I think we perhaps all have areas like that, but hopefully we have learned from them.

Ask the Holy Spirit if there are areas in your life where you are being distracted. He will show you, and then you can immediately do something about it. The problem many have is that they allow a distraction to become a habit in their lives. Once a distraction becomes a habit, it becomes much more difficult to break free from.

My wife, Pam, has been my partner in ministry from the very beginning, and not only is she my wife, but she is also my very best friend. There is no one I trust more than her. I know she loves Jesus more than anything, and I know she is extremely discerning in her spirit.

Everyone needs someone that you are always open to their input. You know they always have your best interests at heart because they are always seeking the to hear from the Holy Spirit.

My wife tries to help me not be distracted, and if I let her, she does a good job. Sometimes I am a little difficult for her to handle, but thank God she continues to try. She never gives up on me, even when I have.

I have a tendency sometimes to live a little on the edge. Probably not too smart, but anything involving a little danger has never seemed to bother me. As a matter of fact, I find it exciting and stimulating, and even restful, to walk on the beach during a violent thunderstorm. Sleeping or resting on my hammock at home in the midst of a storm is also exciting. Now you can see why I need a wife like Pam.

Sometimes I have a tendency (not a good one), to dismiss quickly people who have discernment that perhaps we shouldn't be doing something that I think we should be doing, unfortunately, sometimes even my wife. (Not a good idea.) I especially dismiss input if I think a person is being fearful.

An example of ignoring good sound spiritual advice happened a few years ago in St. Petersburg, Russia. We had traveled there to join a group from Victory Christian Center in Tulsa. Pastors Billy Joe and Sharon Daugherty were doing a crusade there, and my wife and I went along to plant two churches as part of the outreach.

Everything went well, and it was an awesome outreach with Pastors Billy Joe and Sharon ministering to thousands of people giving their hearts to Jesus and many, many healings.

The entire group from Victory in Tulsa was scheduled to leave the day before Pam and I were to leave. Not really sure why or how that happened, but it didn't really matter to me.

We planted the first church, ministered, and saw people saved and healed. It was very exciting. I was ready to see it happen again when we planted the second church, scheduled the day after the Victory Tulsa group left. I was really excited about all that was taking place. I didn't realize it at the time, but I was beginning to get a little distracted. You'll see how it all unfolded shortly.

Pam had asked me earlier if we couldn't leave with the group from Victory Tulsa since she and I would be the only ones left from the group in Russia. I quickly told her there was no problem with our staying, but in her spirit she was troubled.

I never really entertained my wife's concern about our being alone in Russia. Actually, it sounded a little exciting to me. Not too smart.

The day the group left we planted a church in an outlying area, and it was a great day. We met the new pastor at the facility, dedicated the church, and prayed for the people. Truly, anyone could have done what we did, but I thought it should be us. It was exciting to be planting the second new church in Russia.

The following morning, we arrived at about 4 a.m. at the St. Petersburg Airport.

This was still the old terminal, and it was winter and very, very cold. I could tell my wife was ready to leave Russia. She was still a little troubled in her spirit that we had not left with the others.

I checked in our bags with the airline, and the lady at the counter asked me if I knew our visa's had expired the day before.

I told her no. I had never really looked at the visa's when we received them. (Not too smart either.)

Pam had a shocked look on her face, and asked what would happen. I responded quickly that it wasn't a big deal. Pam asked the lady at the baggage counter to confirm if it really wasn't a big deal, and the lady very calmly stated that we would find out when we got to Passport Control.

Well, at Passport Control I found out that what I thought was not a big deal was considered by the Russians a big deal. The lady at Passport Control looked over our passports and visas, then called over a Russian soldier who was armed with an AK-47 across his chest. He was not a very happy person, and that is quite an understatement.

He physically forced us out of the baggage area speaking Russian, indicating we must return to the terminal area. I tried to tell him our luggage had already been checked in, and this just infuriated him. Fortunately, a lady who spoke English intervened, but it sure didn't make him any happier.

We stood there for a moment, hoping something or someone was going to help us. Then they returned and threw (yes threw) our luggage at our feet and motioned for us to return to the terminal.

This meant we had to go against the flow of traffic back through the detector area where there was another Russian soldier with also an AK-47 across his chest.

He had obviously been to the same Russian charm school as the first soldier, and he approached us indicating we could not do what the other soldier told us to do.

Finally, the two Russians made eye contact, and they began to seemingly argue about what to do with us. They finally agreed we needed to go to the terminal. As we stood in the almost empty terminal with our luggage, I realized that perhaps I should have listened to my wife.

I really wasn't too sure what to do. I knew the Lord would take care of us, but I wasn't sure how. The terminal was extremely cold, so I thought I would inject a little humor into our situation. I started looking around, and Pam asked me what I was looking for. I told her I was cold, and I was looking for some hot tea. Actually, both were responses were correct, and I even thought, somewhat funny.

By the look on my wife's face, she did not appreciate my humor.

About that time, probably around 6 a.m., we heard the roar of a jet engine, and our plane was the only one leaving at that time. The sound engulfed the entire terminal, and we knew it was our plane getting ready to leave without us.

My wife just looked at me, and the look was one of: "Why didn't you listen to me when I said I think we are supposed to leave a day early with the group?"

Thank God we were able to locate our host through a cell number my wife had. He helped us negotiate with an immigration officer who said he could help us when he finished a game of chess he was engaged in. Now I think that was funny.

We were charged a fine for overstaying our Russian visa, and had to purchase tickets on another airline in order to get out of Russia on that day. The total cost of my distraction from my wife's discernment was approximately three thousand dollars. An expensive lesson.

I have learned the hard way over the years that I need to pay attention when my wife has a check in her spirit or discernment that I don't have. I would like to say I have arrived in this area, but the truth is I think I'm still arriving.

The world is full of distractions today, especially with the explosion of modern technology. Your mind can be totally bombarded with opportunities for distraction but God has given us the power, authority, and dominion over all potential distractions.

If you are living the word of God and being led by the Holy Spirit, there is no distraction the devil or the world system can entice us with that will work. In addition, there is no distraction that we have ever succumbed to that can stop us from moving forward with God's plan for our lives once we recognize what has happened, ask God's forgiveness, learn from the experience, and move on with God, fully realizing that it is truly possible to:

"MAKE THE BEST OF THE REST"

14

FAILING DOES NOT MAKE YOU A FAILURE

In my office at home I have two desk plaques of quotes from two of my favorite athletes. One is from Babe Ruth of the New York Yankees, and the other is from Michael Jordan of the Chicago Bulls.

"Never let the fear of striking out get in your way."

(BABE RUTH 1895-1948)

"I've missed more than 9,000 shots in my career.
I've lost almost 300 games. Twenty-six times I've been trusted
to take the game winning shot and missed. I've failed over
and over and over in my life. And that is why I succeed."

(MICHAEL JORDAN)

Babe Ruth and Michael Jordan, in my opinion were two of the greatest athletes who dominated their respective sports. They both failed numerous times, yet they never stopped trying.

Babe Ruth during his era led the major leagues in home runs until his record was broken by Hank Aaron. Babe Ruth also, for many years led the league in strike outs. I'm sure he never planned to strike out, it just happened.

I have never met Michael Jordan, but I'll bet every one of the 9,000 plus shots he missed, when he took the shot, he thought he could make it. I'm also pretty sure that after every missed shot, he wasn't thinking about missing the next one, he was thinking about making the next shot.

No matter what our profession or direction in life is, all of us have failed at something. Truly, failing does not make us a failure, only quitting and giving up makes us a failure.

I don't believe that this is a negative statement, but the chances are fairly good that all of us may fail at something again in the future. It isn't that we are planning to fail. We are releasing our faith that we will not fail, but sometimes things happen, and we realize that the venture has failed. Now what do we do?

I believe the answer is very simple. Learn from your failure and move on. As I have said earlier in the book, if we all learn from our failures, we should be brilliant by now.

I realize some people might think what I just shared is a lack of faith. They might say that if we are walking by faith we will never fail. Our confession should be that we will never fail. Well, I don't discount what they might say, but it also makes me think of a scene from one of my favorite movies of all time, *Fiddler on the Roof.*

My guess is most of you have seen the movie. The scene I'm referring to is when the star Tevye is delivering milk to some of his people in the local Jewish Russian village. They are all circled around Tevye's milk cart talking about the current political climate in Russia in the early 1900s.

One of the men says to Tevye and the local Rabbi, "Is there a blessing to be said over the Czar?" One of the men shouts quickly, "Yes, may the Czar stay far away from us." Tevye says, "He is right."

Then another man shouts, "No, we should say a blessing for the Czar," and Tevye says, "He is right."

Then another man shouts out, "You said they are both right, they can't both be right," and Tevye says, "And you are right too!"

I always loved that scene. Many times, we can view things from a total right and wrong view, but there are different views people can take that do not make it wrong for them.

I know that by living the word of God by faith, I am going to succeed because God is going before me to prepare the way and meet all my needs. I know that is truth, and we are called to live the truth.

I also know that from time to time, I can miss God, or things can happen that I just don't understand. I know I'm very capable of missing God. There have been times I have felt to move in a certain direction thinking I have heard from God, but then I later realize I had made a mistake. I hadn't heard clearly from God.

Sometimes in my life, I am sure that things are going to work out in a certain way, I release my faith in God and His word believing I have heard from Him, and then it doesn't happen the way I thought it would. Was it a lack of faith, or did I hear wrong?

Like Tevye said, maybe everybody is right. All I know for sure is this; It is possible for me to think I have heard from God, only to realize later that apparently, I had not. God's will is sovereign, but He is still dealing through His creation of imperfect people even though He is perfect.

The scripture that really helps me in situations that just don't work out the way I thought they would is found in the book of Psalms.

"The steps of a good man are ordered by the Lord, and He delights in his way. Though he fall, he shall not be utterly case down; For the Lord upholds him with His hand."

(PSALM 37:23-24)

It has always been an encouragement to me to realize that I do not have to understand everything, but in everything I know that the Lord will direct my steps. I know that His plans are perfect, and we will always succeed when we are following Him.

Life is a great learning experience, and, in every situation, we find ourselves in, the good, bad or ugly, there is something we can learn. I love the word that I have previously shared in this book, but it is so true:

"All things do work for good to those who love God and are according to His purpose."

(ROMANS 8:28)

Sometimes when I think about God's original plan for Adam and Eve and all of their children, and how specific instructions were given, yet God's plan did not work because Adam and Eve would not cooperate by following and living God's word.

I know I have shared this word earlier in the book, but I think it bears repeating, over and over again because it is so powerful:

"Man shall not live by bread alone, but by every word that proceeds from the mouth of God."

(MATTHEW 4:4)

When we miss God, when we fail at something, we should immediately run to God. He loves us, and no matter how many times we fail, He still has a plan. Running from God should never be an option.

I believe it is a favorite tactic of the enemy to try to entice us to run from God when we fail. It is the same thing that happened to Adam and Eve in the garden when they tried to hide from God after they had failed God.

"Adam and his wife hid themselves from the presence of the Lord God among the trees of the garden. And the Lord called to Adam and said to him, 'Where are you?' So, Adam said, 'I

heard Your voice in the garden, and I was afraid because I was naked, and I hid myself.'"

(GENESIS 3:9-10)

Adam and Eve, because of their failure to obey God allowed fear to separate them from God. God knew where Adam and Eve were hiding, He knows everything, and He sees everything. The fear driving Adam and Eve came from the enemy to separate them from God.

How many times have we done the same thing? It has been my experience as a pastor for all of these many years, that when people feel they have failed God, the first thing they want to do is to stay away from God.

That usually means they stay away from church. Instead of running to God, they move in the direction the enemy would like for them to take. I firmly believe when Adam and Eve failed, the devil brought his authority of fear into their lives and the result was they tried to hide from God.

What would have been the outcome for Adam and Eve and all of mankind if they had run to God and begged His forgiveness instead of entertaining sin and running from God to hide?

Think about your relationship as you were, or are, raising your children. If they hid the truth from you, lied to you or ran away from you, your first response would not necessarily be to reward them or forgive them. Your first response would probably be to determine what form of discipline you were going to use to train them.

On the other hand, what would your response have been whenever one of your children came to you and told you what they did, while asking for your forgiveness. I firmly believe if Adam and Eve had immediately run to God, confessing what they had done, that God's response may have been totally different.

Realize that you are a child of God, and that He has a wonderful plan for your life. He desires to show you His plan, and He will supply all of your needs. He wants you to fellowship with Him, learn to hear His voice, and be willing to follow Him wherever He leads you. He has a great life ahead for you.

Our job in serving God is to do everything in our power to be sure we are hearing clearly from Him. There are times in my life when I know I have heard from God, then there are other times I think I have heard from God. Then there are other times when I'm not really sure, but I hope I have heard from God.

I share these three areas regarding myself, because I believe all of us from time to time miss hearing clearly from God. We begin to move forward with something that we later find out wasn't really God's will after all.

I have failed at many ventures in ministry. Some of the failures were times when I thought I had heard God, only to realize later I had not really heard from God at all. I also learned that if I learned from each one of those occasions, I would grow in wisdom and maturity.

I like what Thomas Edison replied when he was asked about the many times his experiments failed to get the results he was looking for.

"Results! Why, man, I have gotten a lot of results!
I know several thousand things that won't work."

(THOMAS ALVA EDISON)

Don't ever allow failure to define you. You are a child of God, created in His image. Through our Lord and Savior, Jesus Christ, we have been given power, authority and dominion. This was God's original intent for all mankind.

It is our job in serving God to know what God's plan is for our lives. Once we know his plan and His purpose, we can move forth with great confidence and faith in Him.

One of my favorite heroes of the Old Testament was Joshua. He had served as an assistant to Moses and had seen many miracles. When Moses died, God positioned Joshua to be in charge, and he gave Joshua great instructions that are still true and powerful for today. God spoke the following to Joshua:

"This Book of the Law shall not depart from your mouth, but you shall meditate in it, day and night that you may observe to do according to all that is written in it. For then you will make your way prosperous, and then you will have good success. Have I not commanded you? Be strong and of good courage. Do not be afraid, nor be dismayed, for the Lord your God is with you wherever you go."

(JOSHUA 1:8-9)

In every battle that Joshua fought he was successful, with the exception of one. Joshua lost the first battle for the Ai. It was a very difficult experience for him, and he cried out to the Lord asking basically what happened. The Lord answered and told him that he had sin in the camp. In addition, Joshua had not consulted God in regard to the battle plan for Ai.

Perhaps Joshua was so busy celebrating His victory at Jericho that he didn't think to ask God what His plan was for the next battle. That can sometimes happen to all of us. Everything we do seems to prosper, and then we forget to continue to consult with the one who is bringing us the prosperity. It is important that we have God's plans in all that we do.

In preparing for the first battle at Ai, Joshua listened to the people. They told Joshua what he should do, and he listened to them and implemented their plan.

This was a tremendous error on Joshua's part. The battle plan was defeated.

As Joshua cried out to the Lord, God spoke to Joshua and informed him he had sin in the camp.

As soon as Joshua got the sin out of the camp, he immediately asked God for His battle plan, and God showed Joshua what to do. I believe the same is true for each of us. Get rid of the sin, and, consult God for His plan. His plan is better that our plan or anyone else's plan.

With the plan given to Joshua by God, success followed. Joshua had been able to humble himself before God, repent, and seek God's direction. What was true for Joshua is still true today for each of us. God has a plan, and if we will just seek Him, He will always give us His plan assuring the victory.

Don't be moved by apparent failure, learn from it. If you get knocked down, get back up quickly, never stay down. Don't feel sorry for yourself. Know that God has a plan for your life, and that plan is one of victory!

You are not a failure. You are designed by God to live a life going from victory to victory. Seek God in every decision following His leading and you will:

"MAKE THE BEST OF THE REST"

15

FINISH STRONG!!!

There have been many books written relating to finishing strong. There is also merchandise available that shares the importance to finish strong. I agree totally with the concept. Regardless of how our life has been up to this point, it is extremely important that we do everything in our power to finish strong.

Any track star will tell you that as they approach the finish line, it is no time to conserve energy, but it is the time to give it all you have. To finish the race at your top speed with nothing held back.

How do we finish life strong? What is it we can do to make a maximum impact for God?

Regardless of what age you are, I believe it is really important to determine that you have received Jesus Christ as your Lord and Savior, embraced the infilling power of the Holy Spirit to lead and guide you, and have asked God to show you what He wants you to accomplish with the rest of your life.

In the world today most people go to school until they graduate from high school, then many go on to college hoping to eventually find a good job where they make a great deal of money. Then they marry, buy a home, raise a family work hard, retire, and look back over their life. Hopefully they will have made a difference in the world.

I believe God has a plan for every person, and it is as we draw close to Him that we begin to hear what He has for us to accomplish. In our modern age of accelerated growth, I think fewer and fewer people are really seeking the leading of the Holy Spirit in their lives. Too many people have taken over their own lives and are making their own decisions apart from God.

Many times, I ask people the following two questions:

1. What would you do with the rest of your life if you knew you couldn't fail?

2. What would you do with the rest of your life if you had all finances needed?

The various responses I get are very interesting, but one thing I do find in common with many people. They are pursuing doing something they don't really want to do for the rest of their lives. It's hard, almost impossible, to finish strong if you aren't really doing what God has called you to do.

It was almost thirty-nine years ago when I felt the Holy Spirit leading me to Tulsa. The word I had from the Lord was, *"Go to Tulsa and you'll find the meaning for your life."*

I don't believe that God necessarily moves us from one area of the country to another, but I do believe He is continually trying to get our attention to show us what His plan is for our life. It takes a concentrated effort to really listen to the still small inner voice of the Holy Spirit.

When I think about finishing strong, I can't help but think about Pastor Stanley Lo Nathan, who I described in Chapter 11. The story he shared with me regarding the leading of the Holy Spirit in his life is very inspirational. Someday I am hoping he will write a book.

As I shared earlier Pastor Stanley gave his life to the Lord in Cairo after meeting a lady who had started a Bible school there. It was there that Stanley began to learn and grow in the word of God and the leading of the Holy Spirit.

During this time frame Stanley had an opportunity to immigrate to Canada where he would have a job provided in addition to a home. It was an excellent opportunity extended by the government of Canada. They needed more workers in their nation, and they had reached out to many in the Sudan because there were so many displaced Sudanese due to the terrible warfare that had been going on for so many years.

At first Stanley had felt to go, but he was also attempting to follow the leading of that still small inner voice of the Holy Spirit. While the opportunity to migrate to Canada was very tempting, he began to feel that God had something else for him. He began to pray and fast for direction.

It was then that the Lord spoke to him in Cairo asking if Stanley would return to the Sudan to reach out to his people. Once Stanley realized it was the Lord speaking to him, he began to make plans to return to the Yei, Sudan area.

God also began to place a vision in his heart for the precious orphans in the area. I believe orphans, and children in general, have always had a special place in Stanley's heart. I love to watch him interact with children. He loves them, and they love him.

During this period of time when Stanley was receiving his instructions to return to the Sudan, he was also receiving the vision of what eventually became the Dreamland Children's Home in Yei, Sudan.

There was still tremendous fighting going on throughout the south of the Sudan, planes from the north were flying into the south to drop bombs, there was fighting on the ground, and all of this was causing a tremendous food shortage in addition to creating many orphans. One of the worst scenarios of war is the tremendous number of orphans it creates.

Stanley answered the call from God to return to Yei and pursue the vision, and his travel took him into Uganda before he could cross over into the Sudan. Because he didn't have any identification, most people didn't at that time in the southern part of the Sudan, Stanley was thrown into a Ugandan prison. His description of the prison was less than flattering.

Eventually he was released to cross over into the southern part of the Sudan, only to be greeted by authorities and questioned because he had no identification. After much interrogation they placed him in prison in the Sudan.

Stanley described this time as a very difficult time with very little food and water.

I don't know about you, but I think right about now I might have been wondering if I had really heard from God. First prison in Uganda, and now prison in the Sudan.

Stanley continued to have hope, knowing that he had heard from God and that God would provide. In other words, he was moved by the leading of the Holy Spirit, and not the fact that he was living in tremendous hardship just for the basic necessities of life.

He was eventually released and was able to relocate into the town of Yei, South Sudan. It was there, were God wanted Stanley, that he began to see the vision and find the land for the Dreamland Children's Home. It was a tremendous walk of faith by a man of God totally focused on the vision he had received from God.

It was several years later when God brought Pastor Stanley and myself together, through what I believe was a divine appointment, in Juba. It was there when I began to feel the call from God to help this man with the vision God had given him.

Sometimes as I think back on the goodness of God, I feel overwhelmed. One of the things Stanley shared with me was how he had been a heavy drinker in Cairo. He described it as a serious drinking problem, but when the Lord came into his life, he gave it up.

What would have happened to Stanley and the Dreamland if he hadn't gone back to the Sudan from Cairo? What would have happened to Stanley if the lady hadn't started the Bible school in Cairo? What would have happened if I hadn't gone to Tulsa, to Lafayette, to the Sudan? What if?

I believe the greatest experience you can have in your life is to know that you hear from the Holy Spirit of God, and that He has a plan and a purpose for your life. He will begin to direct our steps if we will allow Him, and at the right time He will show us the vision He has for us. Wow! So exciting to know that God wants to use us.

Regardless of what your age is, I can assure you God has a plan for your life. He knows the future He has planned for you, and it will be a wonderful, rewarding experience.

I often wonder if God had someone else that He could have used if I hadn't agreed to follow His leading. My guess is yes, but I'm so glad that he didn't have to find someone else to do what He had called me to do. It has been exciting.

The world is a very busy place, and it will place demands on your time and keep you busy for the rest of your life. Situations and circumstances are everywhere, and people are busy, busy, busy, but busy doing what?

I ask an important question of myself, and I leave the question for you to ask yourself also: Am I busy doing what God has called me to do, or am I just busy? My hope and desire for you is that you are busy doing what God has called you to do.

It takes faith to run the race God has for us, and if you are running that race you know how important it is to you and to God. If you aren't running the race God has for you, all you have to do is ask. Ask God what He would like for you to do with the rest of your life. He will show you.

It takes faith to pursue what God has for us to accomplish for His glory. The Apostle Paul was probably the least likely candidate to pursue God's plan and write two thirds of the New Testament, but on the road to Damascus he encountered the Son of God, Jesus Christ, and his life was changed forever.

It has been almost forty years since God answered my prayer of faith for a wife. Pam has been my partner in marriage and ministry, and I am so blessed by the miracle that she has been to me.

I was a little rough around the edges (that is an extreme understatement) when we came together, but she has always saw things in me that I never saw in myself.

Pam's love for Jesus and her love for me has been a continual encouragement, and her faith in God and her faith in me has always made me a better person.

From the very beginning of our marriage, God told us that it would be His love in our marriage that would minister to others. We have watched God do this. (I have God's word on this recorded in my 1981 prayer journal.)

Let your faith in God and your love for God consume you and flow to others. There are so many hurting people who need to be touched by the love of Jesus flowing through each of us.

We need to focus on finishing strong by encouraging people that no matter what they have experienced in their past, through Jesus, they can make the rest of their life the best of their life.

Paul's words are an encouragement to all of us as he reached the end of his earthly time just before his transition to heaven.

"I have fought the good fight, I have finished the race, I have kept the faith."

(2 TIMOTHY 4:7)

Run the race that God has for you and finish strong. Don't let anything hold you back. Every experience you have had in your life up to the present will be used by God to help you and strengthen you so that you can:

"MAKE THE BEST OF THE REST"

SUMMARY AND YOUR FUTURE

As I stated in the introduction, it is my hope that this book has encouraged, exhorted, and edified you to fulfill your God given destiny during your time on earth.

HOMEWORK ASSIGNMENT

What do you believe God has called you to do with the rest of your life for His glory? If you aren't sure you have definitely heard this from God, what would you like to do with the rest of your life that would bring glory to God?

Get a notebook and begin writing the plan. It will be a fascinating adventure.

(Read Habakkuk 2:2-4 and John 16:13-15)

YOUR TIME LEFT ON EARTH

100 Year Life Span (A Goal for Many)	120 Year Life Span (Genesis 6:3)
0-25............1st Quarter	0-30............1st Quarter
26-50..........2nd Quarter	31-60........2nd Quarter
51-75..........3rd Quarter	61-90..........3rd Quarter
76-100........4th Quarter	91-120........4th Quarter

HOW MANY YEARS DO YOU HAVE LEFT ON YOUR EARTH CYCLE?

100 Year Earth Span.....................................100

Your Current Age.................................. - _____

Your Remaining Years............................ = _____

120 Year Life Span.....................................120

Your Current Age.................................. - _____

Your Remaining Years............................ = _____

"MAKE THE BEST OF THE REST"

WOULD YOU CONSIDER PLANTING A SEED TO HELP AN ORPHAN?

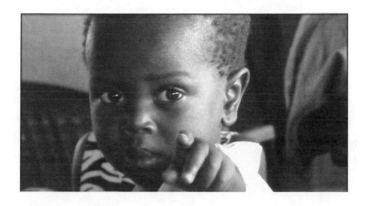

Victory World Outreach is a 501(c)(3) non-profit ministry founded by Pastors Bill and Pam Mickler with a vision to financially assist those who are caring for the orphans of the world. It is estimated that there are approximately one hundred and fifty million orphans in the world.

If you would like to plant a seed, please make your check payable to Victory World Outreach. Mailing instructions are as follows:

Victory World Outreach
Post Office Box 5775
Lafayette, Indiana 47903

You may also give online at:

Dreamland Children's Home
victorylafayette.org/missions

Bill and Pam Mickler
Founding Pastors
Victory World Outreach
Victory Christian Center

Sharing the Love of Jesus with the World
Go and Do Likewise

www.VictoryWorldOutreach.org | P.O. Box 5775 | Lafayette, Indiana 47903

Bill Mickler
billmickler@victorylafayette.org
765-412-3913

Pam Mickler
pammickler@victorylafayette.org
765-426-7597

"Assuredly, I say to you, inasmuch as you did it to one of the least of these My brethren, you did it to Me." (Matthew 25:40)

A FINAL WORD

My friend, thank you for reading this book. I pray that it has been an encouragement to you. You are important to God. He loves you, and He has a plan for your life. This was very difficult for me to grasp, but I thank God for the people who continually encouraged me.

Perhaps at this time you aren't sure what God's plan is for your life. I can relate. Even after I had received Jesus and started attending Bible school, I still didn't know what God's plan was for my life. Don't be discouraged if you aren't sure. He will eventually show you.

In the meantime, get involved with a church that teaches the word of God and embraces the power of the Holy Spirit. The Holy Spirit will eventually reveal to you the plan God has for the rest of your life. This is why the rest of your life will be the best of your life.

Find someone who does know what God has shown them to do with their life and help them. It will be rewarding for them and it will be rewarding to you, and, be sure you are continually carrying a prayer journal. The Holy Spirit can begin speaking to you at any time, and you need to be prepared to write it down.

God loves you, and so do I. Now go forth and:

"MAKE THE BEST OF THE REST"

PASTOR BILL MICKLER INFORMATION

Pastors Bill and his wife Pam are the Founding Pastors of Victory Christian Center Church in Lafayette, Indiana with the vision of "Sharing the Love, Acceptance and Forgiveness of Jesus with Everyone."

Victory World Outreach is a ministry they have also founded to reach the orphans of the world with the vision of "Sharing the Love of Jesus with the World: Go and Do Likewise." The current focus is the South Sudan.

In addition, they serve as Indiana State Directors for Christians United for Israel.

Bill and Pam were Directors of Victory Bible Institute and Victory Fellowship of Ministries in Tulsa, Oklahoma under the leadership of Pastors Billy Joe and Sharon Daugherty.

Bill and Pam have traveled to many nations of the world sharing the love, acceptance and forgiveness of Jesus. They are the proud parents of six children, twelve grandchildren, and four great-grandchildren.

Bill is a Victory Bible Institute graduate, attended Purdue University and is a United States Marine Corps Veteran.

Additional information regarding the ministry of Pastors Bill and Pam Mickler and Victory Christian Center of Lafayette is available as follows:

victorylafayette.org
billmickler@victorylafayette.org

Victory Christian Center
P.O. Box 5177
Lafayette, Indiana 47903

(765) 447-7777 (Church)